Let My People Go!

The Struggle
of the American Jew
to Come Home to Israel

Final Warning - after Wall Street Crash of 2008 8th Edition

By Tom Hess

ISBN 965-7193-16-8

Published by Progressive Vision International

Printed in USA

Dedication and Acknowledgements

This eighth edition of "Let My People Go" is dedicated to the G-d of Abraham. Isaac and Jacob, my closest friend, my Lord and my King. Only by His strong encouragement and grace were we able to complete "Let My People Go" and prepare this eighth edition. This book is also dedicated to the Jewish people in the USA, many who have received and will receive this book as a gift. We have been fasting for *Aliyah* (return to Israel) during the season of Passover for twenty years. In particular, we have called Esther Fasts over the last two Passovers, the three days following the eve of the Passover Seder for *Aliyah* of the Jews to Israel. We plan to continue doing this until ALL the Jewish people return to their land and their G-d, until Messiah comes. (Ezekiel 39:28) We call Christians in all nations to join us in prayer and fasting for protection and deliverance of the Jewish people from anti-Semitism and for the way to be prepared for their *Aliyah* to Israel and to G-d. We hope whoever hears this call will join in this fast. The eighth edition of this book was published in Jerusalem, in obedience to Isaiah 2:3:

The law shall go forth from Zion and the word of the Lord from Jerusalem.

There are now close to one million copies of this book (all editions) in print in thirty languages. We pray this eighth edition in English with the seven hundred scriptures from the Jewish Bible (*Tenach*) on *Aliyah* and the new 13th chapter will increasingly help to spark and kindle a fire that will grow and encourage a massive *Aliyah* movement especially from the USA and the West to Israel. We especially pray for a growing desire among the Jewish people to leave the fleshpots of America to seek, know, praise and worship the G-d of Abraham, Isaac and Jacob in their homeland Israel. We welcome you home to Jerusalem and Israel, the covenantal promised land of Abraham. With the help of the G-d of Israel, you are more than able to possess the Land of Israel, to prepare the way for the Glory of the Lord to be revealed. (Isa. 40:3-5)

Tom Hess

Jerusalem, Israel

January 2010

Foreword

Tom Hess has written a marvelous book of a special importance to the Global Jewish community. He cites the five books of Moses as well as the prophetic writings of the 24 books of the Bible to demonstrate how crucial it is that Jews throughout the world come to live in the State of Israel. Anyone who believes in the sacredness of the Word of God has got to find this book compelling. I would hope that many thousands of Jews will act on the message of this book.

Rabbi Shlomo Riskin, Efrat Israel

Table of Contents

The Struggle of the American Jew to Come Home to Israel

In Isaiah 49:15-16, G-d says He will not forget the Jewish people, but has engraved them on the palms of His hands and their walls are continually before Him!

> **Then say to Pharaoh, "This is what the LORD says: Israel is my firstborn son, and I told you, 'Let my son go, so he may worship me.' But you refused to let him go; so I will kill your firstborn son" (Exodus 4:22-23).**

> **Therefore, say to the Israelites: "I am the LORD and I will bring you out from under the yoke of the Egyptians. I will free you from being slaves to them, and I will redeem you with an outstretched arm and with mighty acts of judgement" (Exodus 6:6).**

LET MY PEOPLE GO! is written to communicate the deep, continual and abiding love G-d has for the Jewish people. He says He will not forget them but has engraved them on the palms of His hands and that their walls are continually before Him. It is because of His love that He always warns them of danger and prepares those who are willing to follow Him in His ongoing purposes throughout history.

Today in America, as G-d's purposes in history are moving onward toward Jerusalem, He is again manifesting His love to His Jewish people. He desires to deliver them from the bondages by which the American culture has entangled them. G-d in His loving-kindness and faithfulness is warning the Jewish people to escape the judgement and plagues coming upon America, and the world.

LET MY PEOPLE GO! is directed toward the American Jew, but the message and warning applies to the whole world. The decadence of

American society has spread throughout the world through mass media. However, due to the size of the American Jewish community in relation to the Jewish communities in other countries, this book is particularly directed toward them. It should be kept in mind though that all sin will be judged and that no culture or society will be exempt.

Just as they were in Egypt, the Jewish people today are in slavery to many false G-ds in America. Many American Jews and Christians have not been aware that they are enslaved by a materialistic system and consequently have not had a desire to be freed. Plagues and judgement are already coming on the G-ds of our contemporary society. My prayer is that the American Jewish people become aware of the bondages to these G-ds and break free from them. They must make *Aliyah* (return) to Israel before greater judgement or plagues come upon America. The Jewish people in America must be freed from this slavery to materialism in all of its forms in order to escape to Israel. Because of the way the Jewish people have prospered and been blessed in America, this struggle is even greater than it was to leave Europe more than seventy years ago. Christians in America need to fast and pray, as did the city of Nineveh, for G-d to stay judgement, for a national spiritual awakening and for the Jewish people to come home to Israel.

LET MY PEOPLE GO! is written to both the Jewish and Christian people, particularly in America and Israel, to help them perceive how G-d has used them together in the past and how G-d's Divine purpose is sovereignly joining them together at this critical time in history. There are obvious difficulties in trying to communicate this message to both communities at the same time because of the different terminology and concepts used by each. While this book attempts to do just that, it offers a unique opportunity for the two communities to dialogue and better understand each other.

While this is a message in love warning the Jewish people to escape the coming judgements on America and follow G-d's call to Israel, it also shows Christian Zionists how they have helped the Jewish people in the past and should help in this coming return.

LET MY PEOPLE GO! was also written out of an alarming vision and growing concern over this struggle for freedom by the more than six million Jewish people in North America. Though some rationalists are not inclined to believe in visions, many are recorded in the Bible. The Prophet Joel said:

> **And afterward, I will pour out my Spirit on all people. Your sons and daughters will prophesy, your old men will dream dreams, your young men will see visions (Joel 2:28).**

On March 19, 1987, G-d spoke into my spirit that judgement was at the door in America. Then on March 24, 1987, as I was sharing and praying with another brother, I had a vision. It seemed as if eternity was at my feet. Bombs were going off over our heads. In the vision, I reached for the phone to call someone and warn them, but it was too late. Suddenly, I found myself praying against the powers of Communism and Islam. Then eternity seemed to vanish before me. Afterwards a still small voice in my spirit said: "Severe judgements are coming on America soon, but I am holding them back briefly because the Jews have not been adequately warned to return to Israel."

A mandate was given to me by the Lord to "Blow a Trumpet in Zion" and "Sound an Alarm" throughout America in love, warning the Jewish people to immediately return to Israel. Also, I was instructed to encourage the Christian Zionists in America to pray for, to warn and to help the Jewish people return to their promised land.

The months of my life after I received this message were very difficult. My work had been one of praying for America (coordinating a 24-hour prayer watch at the steps of the Supreme Court and Capital buildings and leading prayer teams to Israel and other nations to pray) and editing a newspaper committed to building bridges between Jews and Christians. I had a deep love and appreciation for my homeland, America, and for how she has helped the Jewish people. I was also grateful to the Jewish people and Israel, having benefitted greatly from their culture, religion and friendship. I don't know why G-d gave me this message, since I am neither Jewish nor an expert in these matters. Sharing this word has been a struggle, but I must speak out because of my deep love for the Jewish people.

My concern and burden should in no way be taken as anti-Semitic or as disregard for my Jewish brethren. I reject wholeheartedly the ancient stereotype of the Jew as a materialistic and greedy person. Instead, I am showing how the Gentile nation of America has become materialistic and greedy. Both Jew and Christian are being defiled by the influences in this society. I could just as easily write a book specifically warning the Christians in America to live G-dly lives and be a light to the world.

My burden, however, is to be a voice crying in the wilderness that the Jewish people should follow the biblical call and return to Israel, even as I now live in Israel. Israel is not a national ghetto as some would accuse me of saying, but as Isaiah 11:12 says; "He will raise a banner for the nations!"

LET MY PEOPLE GO! was written to help give progressive vision and hope to the Jewish people. Many Jewish people have not returned to Israel because of a lack of knowledge and vision in regard to the *Torah* and G-d's ongoing purposes in history, calling them back to the land.

Where there is no vision, the people perish (Proverbs 29:18 KJV).

To receive G-d's vision for the return of the Jewish people, I encourage you to read, pray, and meditate on the seven hundred scripture verses included in Appendix A of this book. If the Jewish people take these seven hundred scriptures that promise and call them back to the land of Israel, as seriously as many people take scriptures on prospering materially, G-d will soon give them the vision to return with His blessing to their promised land. If they ignore these commands and promises, they may lose what they have and return as refugees or perish in the Diaspora.

LET MY PEOPLE GO! was written recognizing the multifaceted dimensions of this struggle. We recognize the difficulties in breaking from greed, materialism and other false G-ds of our American culture. We must embrace the loving G-d of Abraham, Isaac and Jacob and His biblical call to return to the land of promise. We also recognize the difficult struggle it is to consider breaking from one's family, community and cultural ties when they have been settled in a country for decades, or in some instances, generations.

While it is a struggle for young or elderly Jewish people, it is even *more* difficult for middle-aged Jewish families who are in the prime of life and have bought houses, established vocations and put their children in schools. When the children of Israel left Egypt and Babylon, and more recently when they left Europe, they had to struggle with many of these same difficulties.

Through prayer and determination to follow the call of the G-d of Israel to the land, we can break from these false G-ds and overcome these obstacles. The Jews can be present-day Joshuas and Calebs returning to and possessing the land of promise to worship G-d. Moving to Israel can be difficult because of inevitable tensions and cultural changes to overcome, such as dealing with the bureaucracy and red tape in a culture that does things much slower than America. Things like the school system, banking systems or medical systems can seem less efficient. However, a massive *Aliyah* movement from America to Israel could create an alternative to challenge the cumbersome Israeli bureaucracy.

The possibility of having fewer luxuries, making considerably less money for the same job, paying very high taxes, and in some cases leaving your family and relatives behind can indeed be a sacrifice! Also, the difficulties of the Arab-Jewish conflicts in the land could stop the Jewish people from returning today.

These are, however, minimal difficulties and sacrifices compared to those Joshua, Caleb and the early pioneers faced. They spent decades in the wilderness and once they arrived, still had to conquer the Canaanites before they could possess the land of promise.

The rebirth and restoration of the land in this century already have been pioneered by David Ben Gurion, Golda Meir and many others. Consequently, we should recognize that the struggle for the American Jews to come home to Israel should be less difficult than at any other time in history. Following G-d's call to return to the land in order to worship is the high calling and destiny of the Jewish people. Don't miss your destiny!

LET MY PEOPLE GO! echoes a prophetic command to release the Jewish people to the promised land to worship G-d! It is the command which Moses proclaimed to Pharaoh three thousand years ago. It is the same declaration that must be made today to the G-d of materialism and other false G-ds in America who have gripped both Jew and Christian. Moses commanded Pharaoh to "LET MY PEOPLE GO!, that they may worship G-d!" Although Wall Street is not the main thing that keeps the Jewish people in America, it exemplifies the system the Jews must break from in order to make *Aliyah* to Israel. We should speak to the G-d of materialism in America to give up the Jewish people. To Wall Street we should cry out, "LET MY PEOPLE GO!"

A Jewish lawyer from New York, Shabtai Alboher, who recently made *Aliyah*, was quoted by the *Jerusalem Post* in an article entitled "Slavery in America": "Jewish people in Israel should also go to the American Embassy in Tel Aviv and speak on behalf of the release of the American Jews, as Moses did to Pharaoh, saying: 'LET MY PEOPLE GO!'"

LET MY PEOPLE GO! is a loving prayer for the release and return of the Jewish people. We have begun an International House of Prayer in Jerusalem and also a continual fast for the release of the American Jews. Other groups will be coming to Jerusalem for a week or two each year to pray. We have established this 24-hour Praise and Prayer Watch in Jerusalem where people have been praying around the clock for the return of the Jews from America, and Russia and all nations.

We will also pray for the peace of Jerusalem, the blessing and healing of the nations and the coming of the Messiah. This watch in Jerusalem is based on Isaiah 62:6-7 which says: *"I have posted watchmen on your walls O Jerusalem; they will never be silent day or night. You who call on the Lord, give yourselves no rest, and give him no rest till he establishes Jerusalem and makes her the praise of the earth."* I will be travelling in America, warning the Jews to return and helping them in any way possible.

Our hope is that as G-d works through the message of this book and the continual prayers and fastings of His people, a massive *Aliyah* movement to Israel will take place, not only from Russia, but also from America and other countries.

This book is to say: "Jewish people, you are greatly loved and you are not alone in this struggle. We will struggle together with you in prayer, warning and helping in this return. May you break from the materialistic culture of America and win the struggle to come home to Israel before it is too late. May you return to worship G-d and enjoy Him forever in your land."

Civilizations Warned Before Judgement

Surely the nations are like a drop in a bucket; they are regarded as dust on the scales; he weighs the islands as though they were fine dust. Lebanon is not sufficient for altar fires, nor its animals enough for burnt offerings. Before him all the nations are as nothing; they are regarded by him as worthless and less than nothing (Isaiah 40:15-17).

Do you not know? Have you not heard? Has it not been told you from the beginning? Have you not understood since the earth was founded? He sits enthroned above the circle of the earth, and its people are like grasshoppers. He stretches out the heavens like a canopy, and spreads them out like a tent to live in. He brings princes to naught and reduces the rulers of this world to nothing. No sooner are they planted, no sooner are they sown, no sooner do they take root in the ground, than he blows on them and they wither, and a whirlwind sweeps them away like chaff (Isaiah 40:21-24).

Surely the Lord G-d will do nothing, but he revealeth his secrets unto his servants the prophets (Amos 3:7 KJV).

Eighty-eight major civilizations of man, according to J.D. Unwin, have come and gone since the beginning of time. Each has begun with a strict code of sexual and moral conduct and moral passion. Every society that extended sexual permissiveness and materialistic hedonism was soon to perish: the Babylonian, Persian, Roman, Greek and British Empires are a few examples.

The nations have been warned and judged to varying degrees, but all ceased to be the leading civilizations of their time. The downfall of civilizations often precipitated a new era in history in the timetable of G-d. For example, exactly forty years (one generation), from the beginning of Jesus' ministry to 70 A.D., Jerusalem was destroyed and G-d began working in an increasingly revelatory way among the Gentiles.

Today, as we are at another turning point in history, one cannot help but wonder how much more time the Jewish people have to return. When one looks at the number forty as it relates to judgement throughout history, it seems as though the Diaspora Jews may currently be living on borrowed time.

G-d told Jonah that Nineveh would be destroyed in forty days. The flood lasted forty days and forty nights and destroyed the whole world. During the first Exodus, the unbelieving Israelites who despised the Promised Land missed their destiny and wandered in the desert for forty years. The law was given to Moses in forty days but at the end of that forty days, judgement fell on the camp for their sin.

Before both temples were destroyed, G-d gave the Jewish people forty years of grace to rethink their ways. Ezekiel lay on his side for forty days, one day for each year, bearing the sin of Judah. Then forty years after the Kingdom of Israel went into exile in Assyria, Jerusalem was destroyed. Forty years after the Sanhedrin moved from the temple to the marketplace, and forty years after Jesus warned of coming destruction, the temple and Jerusalem were destroyed. If in the first and second Jewish states G-d granted forty years of grace, how much time will He give in the third?

Throughout biblical history, living in the land of Israel meant living in the abundance of G-d's blessings. Deuteronomy 28:8 says: "The LORD your G-d will bless you in the land He is giving you." Yet, fifty-five years after the rebirth of Israel most of the Diaspora Jews have not heeded G-d's call to come home. Just how much longer do they have?

At this, the printing of the Seventh Edition of *LET MY PEOPLE GO!* in 2004, we have entered the fifty-fifth year of Israel, the year of double grace. Isaiah 61:1 says this is the year to proclaim freedom for the captives. I believe we are about to see a much greater *Aliyah* from the USA and all nations in the coming years!

In October 1987, at the beginning of the fortieth year on the Hebrew calendar, a few of us were praying in our house of prayer in Jerusalem. Within a few weeks time an earthquake hit Los Angeles and in New York City the stock market fell a record 508 points in one day. These events could be warning signs of coming judgements on America and the Gentile nations.

Since the first printing of the book in 1987, we have seen over one million Jews come home from Russia and the North as well as from the South and East, and in 2002 *Aliyah* began to break open from the West. It seems as if we are approaching the end of the times of the Gentiles and the cloud of Glory is beginning to lift from the civilization in America and is moving again toward Jerusalem. We are coming full circle to where all roads lead back to Jerusalem, the City of the Great King for the final civilization of man!

After nineteen hundred years of being under Gentile rule, Jerusalem and Israel have both been brought back under Jewish rule. Isaiah 11:11-12 says:

> **In that day the Lord will reach out his hand a second time to reclaim the remnant that is left of his people from Assyria, from Lower Egypt, from Upper Egypt, from Cush, from Elam, from Babylonia, from Hamath and from the islands of the Sea. He will raise a banner for the nations and gather the exiles of Israel; he will assemble the scattered people of Judah from the four quarters of the earth.**

As the Jewish people consider the struggle to escape to Israel, may they remember that throughout history G-d has warned civilizations that have rejected Him to worship other G-ds. Scripture describes some of these G-ds as materialism (golden calf), sex (fertility G-ddesses), abortion (child sacrifice to Molech), and atheism (man or self). Only after warning and a call to repentance does judgement come upon them.

In most instances in history, when major judgements come on civilizations, as many believe could soon happen to America and other Gentile nations (Jeremiah 30:11), less than ten percent of the Jewish people have escaped. The following are some biblical and historical warnings, types of deliverances, responses and judgements:

THE FLOOD – *(Noah gave warning)* Only Noah and seven others were saved out of the entire world population. The whole world was destroyed by the flood after Noah warned them for a hundred and twenty years and built an ark for their deliverance.

SODOM AND GOMORRAH – *(Angels gave warning)* Four were saved out of the entire population of Sodom and Gomorrah and one of them was destroyed by becoming a pillar of salt. Angels warned Lot to take his family and anyone else in the city who belonged to him and flee immediately, then G-d destroyed these wicked cities and people by fire and brimstone from heaven. More than forty years ago, before abortion was legalized or AIDS was even thought of, Billy Graham said that if G-d would not destroy America for her sins, He would have to apologize to Sodom and Gomorrah! How much more so now!

1200-1500 B.C. – *(Moses gave warning)* Moses warned the Egyptian Pharaoh to let G-d's people go, but Pharaoh pursued the Israelites and was destroyed. This precipitated the downfall of the Egyptian civilization.

862 B.C. – *(Jonah gave warning)* Jonah told the people of Nineveh that they would be destroyed in forty days. All the people fasted and prayed and G-d delayed destruction for more than one hundred years.

721 B.C. – *(Hosea and Isaiah gave warning)* The Northern Kingdom of Israel fell to the Assyrians and the Israelites were scattered throughout Assyria. Hosea and Isaiah, among others, had rebuked Israel's idolatrous and corrupt ways and warned of this destruction.

586 B.C. – *(Jeremiah and Isaiah gave warning)* Judah and its capital, Jerusalem, surrendered to Babylonian control after the warnings of Jeremiah and Isaiah fell on deaf ears. The Jews were taken into exile to Babylon.

539 B.C. – *(Daniel gave warning)* Babylon was captured in one night when the Persian leader Cyrus stepped into power without a fight. Daniel warned of the end of Babylonian rule when he literally saw the writing on the wall. Only a small percentage were able to flee.

331 B.C. – *(Daniel gave warning)* The Persian Empire, the largest ever seen in the ancient East, fell to Alexander the Great in one decisive battle. Daniel warned of the end of Persian rule.

133 B.C. – *(Daniel gave warning)* The Greek Empire fell to Rome, and the Roman Empire united the then known world under their rule. Daniel also warned of the division and end of the Roman Empire.

70 A.D. – *(Jesus gave warning)* Jesus warned the Jewish people in 33 A.D. of the soon coming destruction of Jerusalem (Matthew 23:37 and Matthew 24:2). Jerusalem was destroyed in 70 A.D. by Titus, the Roman Commander. Some one and a half million Jewish people were killed according to Josephus.

(G-d supernaturally gave warning) According to Josephus, G-d then warned the Jewish people immediately preceding the attack in 70 A.D. by having a sword appear over the City of Jerusalem for about ten days. The first night of the ten days, the Eastern Gate opened supernaturally and one hundred thousand fled, i.e. only seven to ten percent of the population left before its destruction.

1300 A.D. – (Rabbi Nachmanides gave warning) One hundred years prior to the Inquisition, he said destruction was coming to the Jews of Spain. He not only encouraged Jews throughout Spain to make *Aliyah*, but led his followers in making *Aliyah* to Palestine himself!

1920-1944 A.D. – *(Jewish and Christian Zionist Leaders gave warning of the Holocaust)* Rabbis in Europe in the 1920s and 1930s, preceding the Holocaust, were discouraging the Jews from making *Aliyah* and moving back to their home land. However, Vladimir Jabotinsky was going throughout Europe saying: "Liquidate the Diaspora or the Diaspora will liquidate you," and Dr. Max Nordau was saying that only one-third of the Jews would return to the land and the rest would eventually be assimilated or would die in the Diaspora. These and other Zionists were traveling throughout Europe warning the Jews to leave before and during Adolf Hitler's reign of terror because they sensed impending doom. Hardly anyone listened.

Six million Jewish people were destroyed in Germany and Europe. This happened within forty years after the time Herzl founded the World Zionist Congress and when the Christian Zionist, Rev. William Hechler, began to teach from the Bible that G-d would soon restore the Nation of Israel. Hechler also warned that an anti-Semitic movement would come and create in the Jews a longing to return to their land.

While nominal, counterfeit Christians were involved in betraying and destroying the Jewish people in Europe, Christian Zionists were helping the Jewish people. Corrie Ten Boom is one such Christian Zionist whose story is told in the book and film, *The Hiding Place*. Dietrich Bonhoeffer, a famous theologian, was imprisoned and later killed in a plot to try to stop Hitler. Other voices warned of coming tragedy, yet only approximately ten percent or six hundred thousand Jews left!

Unfortunately, the Jews had few places to go in the 1930s since the State of Israel had not yet been established. After this tragedy, and the death of six million Jews, the State of Israel was born. Out of death, G-d has brought new life and hope and has given back to the Jewish people the land of Israel after almost two thousand years. Still, only five and a half million out of the total world Jewish population of thirteen million have followed G-d's call to come home.

1970s A.D. – *(Jewish and Christian Zionists gave warning)* Zionist leaders encouraged Jews from Iran to escape and make *Aliyah* to Israel. Some left, but many stayed and now it is very difficult to leave under the reign of the Ayatollahs.

1977-1983 A.D. – *(Jacob Timmerman gave warning)* A newspaper editor warned Jewish people of coming Nazi anti-Semitism in Argentina (a Western country in South America). Timmerman encouraged Jewish people to return to Israel but few left. He was put under house arrest and greatly tortured. Virtually no other leaders stood with him. The American Press stated that thirty to forty thousand Jews were missing or tortured. Thousands to this day have never been found. Timmerman is another example of G-d's faithfulness to warn people before calamity.

2004 or soon after – *Increasing judgement of* G-d *on America!* *(Will YOU help give the warning?)* As we observe the moral, economical, military and spiritual state of America, we can again see the handwriting on the wall. America's days are numbered as the leading world power. To whom much has been given, much has been required. We have been weighed in the balance and found wanting as a nation.

Servants of G-d have been warning of the coming judgements on America for centuries. During the Revolutionary War, George Washington, the father of our nation, had a vision about the destruction of America before it was even born. This vision is recorded in the Library of Congress. Washington saw the results of the Revolutionary and the Civil Wars and warned of the coming judgement of America in a third war. The following is the third war or peril George Washington saw coming on America:

"The Third Peril

"Again I heard the mysterious voice saying, 'Son of the Republic, look and learn.' At this the dark, shadowy angel placed a trumpet to his mouth, and blew three distinct blasts; and taking water from the ocean, he sprinkled it upon Europe, Asia and Africa. Then my eyes beheld a fearful scene. From each of these continents arose thick black clouds that were soon joined into one. And throughout this mass there gleamed a dark red light by which I saw hordes of armed men. These men, moving with the cloud, marched by land and sailed by sea to America, which was enveloped in the volume of the cloud. And I dimly saw these vast armies devastate the whole country and burn the villages, towns and cities which I had seen springing up.

"As my ears listened to the thundering of the cannon, clashing of swords, and the shouts and cries of swords, and the shouts and cries of millions in mortal combat, I again heard the mysterious voice saying, 'Son of the Republic, look and learn.' When this voice had ceased, the dark shadowy angel placed his trumpet once more to his mouth, and blew a long and fearful blast."

At the beginning of this century, the Christian Zionist, Charles Parham, the father of the Pentecostal movement, warned of judgements coming on America. Referring to James 5 and Washington's vision, Parham stated: "Prophecy states that near the time of the end the Church and nation will become lifted up and forget G-d and spread itself abroad in power and self-glory. For these things G-d will devastate the nation and the whole body of the eagle will be burned, as Washington in his vision toward the end of this nation's history saw cities laid waste from coast to coast."

David Wilkerson, author of the book, *The Cross and the Switchblade* that was the inspiration for the movie of the same name, had a vision and has been warning of a coming nuclear destruction of America for the same reasons.

Similarly, Hal Lindsey, author of the book, *The Late Great Planet Earth*, which inspired the movie of the same name, also has been warning saying: "AMERICA WILL BE DESTROYED BY A NUCLEAR FIRST STRIKE."

These warnings and many others have been given to America as a whole. G-d now seems to be giving a specific warning to the Jewish people in America to return to Israel soon to escape the coming judgement and prepare for the great revival coming to the land of Israel.

At this time, most rabbis and spiritual leaders of Jewish people in America are responding as their counterparts did before the Holocaust in Germany and Europe in the 1920s and 1930s. Many are either discouraging *Aliyah* saying they are American Jews or are not strongly encouraging it because they are building their own movements. Very few are making it a major priority or leading their congregations in massive *Aliyah* to Israel despite the biblical injunction to return to the land. In Appendix A, seven hundred verses of scripture are given which either commanded the Jewish people to return to Israel or which contain promises of G-d's blessings upon His people in this land.

Meanwhile, during the last fifty-five years, Israeli Jewish leaders, including former prime ministers and Jerusalem Mayors Teddy Kollek and Ehud Olmert, have strongly encouraged *Aliyah*. Former Prime Minister Yitzhak Shamir encouraged the leading rabbis of Syria to make *Aliyah* and call all Syrian Jews to Israel and join him in Israel! Prime Minister Ariel Sharon spoke out strongly about *Aliyah* and believes for another million Jews to come to Israel. May thousands of rabbis do the same from Russia, Argentina, Canada, Great Britain, France and the USA.

Many other Israeli Zionist envoys have been encouraging and pleading with the Jewish people in the Diaspora including the well-known Bible teacher, Lance Lambert. Jan Willem van der Hoeven, Jay Rawlings, Steve Lightle, Ulf Ekman, and many other Christian Zionists have also been warning the Jews to return as well.

The next world war will probably be World War III mentioned in Ezekiel 38 and 39, and also referred to as the Gog and Magog War. It appears that the nations of Russia, Sudan, Libya, Germany, and Iran, together representing the forces of the Islamic Revolution and anti-Semitism, may attack and devastate the USA as implied in George Washington's vision. But according to Ezekiel 39, when they come against little Israel, G-d Himself will intervene and destroy them. G-d says He will send fire on Magog and those who live in the coastlands, possibly referring to Russia and America. Little Israel may be devastated but she *shall survive.*

Israel's future is biblically certain. America is not mentioned specifically at all, but many believe America, and in particular New York, is the daughter of Babylon which the book of Revelation says is to be destroyed.

Many Jewish people have believed that Israel's security is in the military and financial support coming from America. The Jewish people need to be warned that while the support of America has in many ways been a blessing in the past, the future support of Israel will increasingly come from G-d Himself and, hopefully, from her loyal Christian Zionist friends around the world.

Psalm 20:7 says some trust in chariots, and some in horses, but we trust in the name of the Lord our G-d! This scripture will become more important and relevant for Israel in the future. She will realize her increasing vulnerability in trusting in America, and her growing need to depend on, and trust in, the G-d who keeps Israel and who neither slumbers nor sleeps (Psalm 121:4).

Much prayer and fasting has moved G-d's hand to bring the end of Communist rule in Russia and the Soviet Union and the resignation of Mikhail Gorbachev at of the end of 1991.

But the fact of the changes and the cry of peace in Russia and elsewhere does not mean that there are not still many nuclear weapons both in Russia, Communist China, Moslem countries and other enemy countries. While people are saying, "Peace and safety," destruction will come on them suddenly as labor pains on a pregnant woman and they will not escape.

Saddam Hussein (now in prison), Muammar Khadafi and other leaders of the Islamic Revolution are obviously satanically inspired and have warned that they are committed to the destruction of America. They have clearly stated their intentions to destroy us.

Some, after reading this book, will say G-d may judge America but they don't think the time is yet. However, it may be sooner than we think. The anti-Messiah world order forces are now launching the most spectacular peace movement on record both in the West and in the East. Don't forget that in every major civilization most people waited too long to prepare to escape and respond for deliverance. Never, to my knowledge, did a falling civilization respond too quickly. Today is the day to hear G-d's voice and respond to what He has for you. Business as usual in America is over for all who have ears to hear.

G-d is warning the Jews of America to make an Exodus from the American civilization to Israel very soon. Israel is to be the next and last civilization of man according to prophecy. It is important that the Jewish people leave America before they get caught in a trap and lose their finances in an economic collapse. They then would go home with nothing, or may get caught in a nuclear holocaust. They would miss their destiny in Israel as six million Jewish people did in Europe earlier in the previous century.

Many Jewish people from Germany and Europe talked about leaving for years before the Holocaust. Sadly, most of them were caught up in the simple cares and anxieties of everyday life. They ignored the warnings and missed the purpose of G-d for them in their generation. May we be thankful for G-d's continual faithfulness and loving-kindness in that throughout history He warned His people when judgements were coming so they could escape.

As the philosopher Santayana said, "He who does not learn from the lessons of history is doomed to repeat them." May the American Jewish people learn from the failure of past generations to heed the faithful warning, call and commandments of G-d to escape to Israel and flee the impending judgements on America. May G-d grant a massive *Aliyah* movement of American Jewish people to break free from the bondage of American materialism and return to the reborn nation of Israel before it is too late. May G-d call home many faithful Jewish people who, as practical Zionists, will help restore Israel to its greatest glory!

3

A Warning of Progressive Judgements on America

The judgements of the LORD are true and righteous altogether (Psalm 19:9 KJV).

Come, O Zion! Escape, you who live in the Daughter of Babylon! (Zechariah 2:7)

A nation from the north will attack her and lay waste her land. No one will live in it; both men and animals will flee away. "In those days, at that time," declares the LORD, "the people of Israel and the people of Judah together will go in tears to seek the LORD their G-d. They will ask the way to Zion and turn their faces toward it. They will come and bind themselves to the LORD in an everlasting covenant that will not be forgotten" (Jeremiah 50:3-5).

G-d's judgement is righteous in that it honors the Holy G-d of Israel who cannot stand sin and it enables Him to purge away the cancer of decay and sin from a civilization, society or world. New York and America, which is believed by some to be the heart of Babylon today, are on the brink of tremendous judgement. September 11th, 2001 was the first-fruit of greater judgement. Unless the Jewish people escape to Israel, they will experience the ever-increasing judgement coming upon America in the next few years! If these increasing judgements do not cause the Jewish people to return to Jerusalem soon, there is little hope they will return!

---

1. *Family Issues Forum*, A Publication of the B'nai B'rith Center for Jewish Family Life, A Conversation with Egon Mayer on Intermarriage, http://bnaibrith.org/f.../fif/aut95/emayer.htm.

Judgement Begins at the Household of G-d

For it is time for judgement to begin with the family of G-d; and if it begins with us, what will the outcome be for those who do not obey the gospel of G-d? (I Peter 4:17)

G-d is judging individuals, ministries and churches. Adulterous affairs that have been going on over the last ten years have been recently exposed. Pride, arrogance and the false G-d of mammon that have seduced many in the Church are being exposed. The doctrine that the Church must become bigger and better is prideful deception. The Church of the future will be more underground due to the persecution and coming financial challenges in our society.

Jewish People in Cults and Jewish Assimilation

Surveys show that up to 15% of those involved in cults in America are Jewish, yet only 2-3% of the total American population is Jewish. Also, more than one million Jewish people in America have been assimilated in the last forty years. The United Jewish Community Survey 2000-2001 reports that 31% of Jews in the US intermarry. The intermarriage rate in the US increased from 6% in 1964, to 14% in 1975, to 23% in 1987, to 38% in the mid-1980's, to 43% in 1990, and as high as 47% since 1996. Portions of families in which non-Jewish spouses converted to Judaism declined from 44% in 1971 to 27% in 1975 to 12% since 1980.[1]

Anti-Semitism Is Increasing

Louis Farrakhan said to a radio audience of ten thousand in Washington, D.C. in 1986, that soon we will be rolling the heads of Jews down the aisles in America! In 1996 he led a million-man march on Washington, D.C. and he has received millions of dollars from Libya's Khadafi and Iraq's Saddam Hussein to accomplish his anti-Semitic purposes. Anti-Semitism is evident

---

1.*Anti-Semetism Worldwide* 2002/3, Tel Aviv University, www.tau.ac.il/Anti-Semetism/asw2002-3/general.htm

2. For Abortion sources see: www.nrcl.org/abortion/aboramt.html

and increasing.

Jewish people could become "scapegoats" if there is a financial collapse in America. Blame would particularly be directed to the Director of the Federal Reserve, Alan Greenspan, and many leading economists who are Jewish.

The Ku Klux Klan, Neo-Nazi movements, and other anti-Jewish groups have been on the rise every year. In 1987, anti-Semitic vandalism increased by seventeen percent in America according to the Anti-Defamation League of B'nai B'rith. Throughout the 1990's Palestinian protests and riots in Israel began, which have caused world opinion to turn increasingly against Israel. In 2002, during the buildup to the second Gulf War, approximately two hundred thousand people gathered in Washington D.C. for the National March for Palestine against War and Racism using anti-Semitic slogans like "End the Holocaust."[1]

Jews are safer in Israel because they are in control of their own security rather than being at the mercy of others. Psalm 121:4 (KJV) says: "He that keepeth Israel shall neither slumber nor sleep."

Economic Judgements

In less than eight years, America has moved from the greatest investing nation to the greatest debtor nation in the world. Also, for the first time, many countries say they will not be able to repay their debts to us. In 2003 the US national debt reached more than $6.9 trillion and continues to increase! Several large companies have put their money in Swiss banks. Monetary and financial collapse may be imminent. Isaiah 60 says that the wealth of the nations is to be gathered and brought to Israel. Unless the Jewish people leave soon, they may have to go back as refugees with nothing.

---

1. UNAIDS Questions & Answers, November 2003, II/1; and UPI 2/04.

Abortion

More than forty million babies have been killed in the last thirty years in America! Exodus 20:13 says: "You shall not murder" ("kill" - KJV), yet the USA has the second most liberal abortion laws in the world! In 1973, the year abortion was legalized, there were 745,000 reported abortions. After a steady climb since 1973, the number of reported abortions in the US rose to 1,608,600 in 1990, but dropped to 1,365,700 in 1996.[2]

There is so much blood on American soil, it is a miracle we have not already been destroyed as a nation! Many secular, reformed and conservative Jews have encouraged abortion despite the fact that the killing of their future generations will affect the future of the Jewish people. There is little difference between child sacrifice in the Old Testament and abortions today.

"For this reason was man created alone, to teach thee that whosoever destroys a single soul of Israel, scripture imputes [guilt] to him as though he had destroyed a complete world; and whosoever preserves a single soul of Israel, scripture ascribes [merit] to him as though he had preserved a complete world." Babylonian Talmud Sanhedrin 37 in Mishna 20

AIDS: A Judgement of G-d on Immorality

Although many are being infected in innocent ways, in the USA there are over two and a half million people who have either died from AIDS, have AIDS, or are HIV positive as of 2003. New York is the largest Jewish city in the world with more than seventy-five thousand people known to have AIDS or infected with HIV, 15% of total AIDS cases in the USA. The high rate is similar to some third world countries in Asia, Central and South America, and Africa. The epidemic is spreading in New York, throughout the USA and other places. There is a very real possibility of innocent people in the main stream of America contracting and dying from AIDS.[1]

---

1. 1995 *Information Please Almanac*, p. 411.
2. Facts on File, World News Digest with Index, 1995, Volume 55, No. 2838, p. 357.

Judgement in Politics and Business

Politicians who have been living in adultery or corruption for decades are being exposed. Past Presidents of the USA have gotten away with this, but not those of today! G-d is judging at this time. President Clinton was caught in a scandalous affair. Business leaders are also being exposed, including Ivan Boesky, Mafia leaders and many others.

Terrorism in the USA

Terror will seize them, pain and anguish will grip them; they will writhe like a woman in labor. They will look aghast at each other, their faces aflame (Isaiah 13:8).

In **1987** the Associated Press reported that the FBI averted two hundred cases of terrorism in America in 1986. Thousands of terrorists are already in America and could strike at any time. Their most likely places to strike are in the larger cities, where most Jewish people live.

1993 - February 26, New York City: A bomb exploded in the basement garage of the World Trade Center, killing six persons and injuring at least a thousand others. It was declared the worst terrorist bombing on US soil.[1]

1995 - April 20, Oklahoma City: A truck-bombing attack on a federal office building left a death toll of 168, including 19 children. In addition, a nurse involved in the rescue operation died of a head injury incurred during the effort. More than four hundred were injured.[2]

2001 - September 11, New York City & Washington D.C.: Two airplanes hijacked by Islamic terrorists crashed into the World Trade Center and Pentagon. In one hour numerous people were injured and about three thousand people were killed. This is more people killed than in all the terrorist attacks in Israel in the last seven years combined.

2004 - Threats of terrorism continue to increase in the US after US involvement in Afghanistan, Iraq and other nations.

---

1. *The World Almanac and Book of Facts 2003*, p.187-192.
2. 1995 *Information Please Almanac*, p. 405.

Erratic Weather Conditions

There will be signs in the sun, moon and stars. On the earth, nations will be in anguish and perplexity at the roaring and tossing of the sea (Luke 21:25-26).

I will show wonders in the heaven above and signs on the earth below, blood and fire and billows of smoke. The sun will be turned to darkness and the moon to blood before the coming of the great and glorious day of the Lord (Acts 2:19-20).

According to these scriptures, there are coming changes in the heavens and the seas. This will affect the health and lives of many people.

1993 - June - August: Two months of heavy rain caused the Mississippi River and its tributaries to flood in ten states (Illinois, Iowa, Kansas, Kentucky, Minnesota, Missouri, Nebraska, North Dakota, South Dakota and Wisconsin), causing almost fifty deaths and an estimated twelve billion US dollars in damage to property and agriculture in the Midwest. Almost seventy thousand people left homeless. **Winter 1996/97**: Devastating floods take twenty-nine lives in the Northwest. **2002** - May: Flooding in Missouri, Illinois, Indiana, West Virginia, Virginia, and Kentucky cause great damage and take twenty lives. **Summer 2002 & 2003**: Wildfires in the West scorched over seven million acres of forested land, destroyed over four thousand homes, killed more than fifty people, and cost four billion US dollars in property damages and fire fighting expenses.[1]

Some of the costliest natural disasters in US history and their total cost (including uninsured losses) are: **1989** - Hurricane Hugo, $5.9 billion (US mainland), **1992** - Hurricane Andrew, thirty billion US dollars, and **1993** - Midwest flooding, twelve billion US dollars.[2]

Famine

No one ever thought there would be severe famine in America, but

---

1. ibid.
2. http://wwwneic.cr.usgs.gov/neis/eqlists/94.lis.

it may come sooner than we think. Weather conditions could affect the crop cycle and bring this about. Oil shortages also could affect delivery of food to population centers. Revelation 18 describes famine as one result of the fall of Babylon. Matthew 24 speaks of famine. Also, Luke 6:25 says, "Woe to you who are well fed now, for you will go hungry."

Earthquakes

More earthquakes shook the world in 1986 than in any other year in history. Seismologists say the earthquake threat is possibly growing and damage potential is greater because of urban expansion. The two major earthquake faults in the world run through the USA and earthquakes could occur in America at any time (Matthew 24:7). The two most likely places for earthquakes are on the East Coast and West Coast where it happens that most Jewish people live. Hundreds of earthquakes have destroyed many people during the history of America.

1989 - San Francisco Bay area earthquake during the World Series: 5.9 billion US dollars (including uninsured losses).[1]

1994 - January 17, Southern California: A 6.8 earthquake struck killing sixty people, more than seven thousand injured, twenty thousand homeless and more than forty thousand buildings damaged in Los Angeles, Ventura, Orange and San Bernardino Counties. Severe damage was caused by collapsed overpasses and fires. Estimates of damage came to be around twenty billion US dollars.[2]

Terrorist and Nuclear, Biological and Chemical Attacks– A Primary Concern of this Book!

Many cities are targeted for terrorist and nuclear attacks and could be destroyed. Most Jewish people live in large cities in the USA, not in the country, and are therefore susceptible to decimation (Isaiah 6:9-13; Revelation 18).

G-d judged the nation of Israel in 70 A.D. Now He is about to judge America and the Gentile nations. The Jewish people need to return to Israel or they could experience a nuclear holocaust! It is time for the American Jewish community to make massive *Aliyah* to Israel before it's too late!

Progressive judgements will come on America in the coming years. Their severity will depend on the degree of repentance in the near future in America. It would take repentance, fasting, prayer and revival as in Nineveh to turn increasing judgements from America. My prayer is that a warning of progressive judgements on America will be taken seriously by the Jewish people.

G-d's purposes and plans in the earth to bring all the Jewish people home to Israel shall be fulfilled, as Ezekiel 39:28 states. The progressive judgements that G-d is bringing on America are righteous and should be received by the Jewish people as a clear warning from a loving G-d that it is time to return to the land of Israel. May the Jewish people be like the sons of Issachar and discern the times in which they live and know what they should do! (I Chronicles 12:32)

As the cloud of glory, in increasing ways, lifts off America and moves back to Jerusalem, so will G-d's favor lift off the Jewish people in America. The Jewish people who do not heed the loving warning of a righteous G-d will probably be greatly devastated or destroyed by the progressive judgements coming on America.

Precious Jewish people, escape the coming judgements on America and possibly a nuclear holocaust. Return to the reborn land of Israel and help restore your nation for the King of Glory!

4

The Rebirth and Restoration of Jerusalem and Israel

Who has ever heard of such a thing? Who has ever seen such things? Can a country be born in a day or a nation be brought forth in a moment? Yet no sooner is Zion in labor than she gives birth to her children (Isaiah 66:8).

Therefore this is what the Sovereign LORD says: "I will now bring Jacob back from captivity and will have compassion on all the people of Israel, and I will be zealous for my holy name. They will forget their shame and all the unfaithfulness they showed toward me when they lived in safety in their land with no one to make them afraid. When I have brought them back from the nations and have gathered them from the countries of their enemies, I will show myself holy through them in the sight of many nations. Then they will know that I am the LORD their G-d, for though I sent them into exile among the nations, I will gather them to their own land, not leaving any behind. I will no longer hide my face from them, for I will pour out my Spirit on the house of Israel," declares the Sovereign LORD (Ezekiel 39:25-29).

G-d initially revealed the Zionist vision to Abraham, and led the Great Patriarch over four thousand years ago to the land of Canaan and to Jerusalem which later became known as "David's City." In 1967, Jerusalem was restored as the capital of the Nation of Israel which was reborn in 1948 and is in the process of being restored. Jerusalem will soon become the Messiah's capital not only for Israel, but for the whole world.

And it shall come to pass in the last days, that the mountain of the LORD's house shall be established in the

top of the mountains, and shall be exalted above the hills; and all nations shall flow unto it. And many people shall go and say, Come ye, and let us go up to the mountain of the LORD, to the house of the G-d of Jacob; and he will teach us of his ways, and we will walk in his paths: for out of Zion shall go forth the law, and the word of the LORD from Jerusalem. And he shall judge among the nations, and shall rebuke many people: and they shall beat their swords into plowshares, and their spears into pruninghooks: nation shall not lift up sword against nation, neither shall they learn war any more (Isaiah 2:2-4 KJV).

The first mention of Jerusalem in the Bible is in Genesis 14:17-24, when Melchizedek, the King of Salem, brought out bread and wine and blessed Abraham, saying: "Blessed be Abram of the most high G-d, possessor of heaven and earth." Almost every time we lead a group of people entering Jerusalem and ascend the hills of Jerusalem, we stop and break bread and wine in remembrance of Melchizedek blessing Abraham and we receive G-d's blessing as spiritual descendants of Abraham. After Abraham's time, famine struck the land, and Abraham's descendants sojourned in Egypt. It was at that time G-d gave Moses the vision to lead the first Exodus out of Egypt, gave the Ten Commandments and established the Tabernacle ritual of sacrifice, bringing tremendous blessing not only upon the children of Israel, but upon all the nations of the world. Then Joshua led the Israelites into the land to possess it.

Almost one thousand years after Abraham, Jerusalem rose to its greatest glory when King David brought the Ark of the Covenant there and the temple was built by Solomon. The Tabernacle of David established the worship of the Lord, using rams' horns, trumpeters, cymbals, dancers, singers, and the playing of lyres and harps. King David danced and celebrated before the G-d of Israel. David wrote most of the Psalms, which are the best songs in the world to this day!

Then idolatry entered the nation and soon G-d's judgement fell. Isaiah warned of this judgement that came through Assyria and then Jeremiah warned of the second blow by the Babylonians. The second return of the

Jews to the land was under the Persian ruler Cyrus. This return brought even greater blessing not only to Israel, but to the whole world. At the end of this time came Jesus' birth and sacrificial death. Then the biblical message spread throughout the world to the Gentiles.

Another watershed year was 1948. Theodore Herzl had prophesied in 1897 that Israel would be formed within fifty years. Exactly fifty years later, after the terrible devastation of the Holocaust, Israel was reborn in 1948. The first page of the *Jerusalem Post* read, "ISRAEL BORN IN A DAY!" (see Appendix B). Ironically, Andre Gromyko, the former Minister for Foreign Affairs and President of the Soviet Union, which then had two million Jewish people bound in slavery, was the first to sign the agreement recognizing Israel as a nation on November 27, 1947.

Not only was Israel reestablished as a nation in 1948, but also the United Nations and the World Council of Churches were formed. Dr. Billy Graham, Dr. Bill Bright, Dr. Richard Halverson and many other evangelical and charismatic ministries also began their ministries then. David du Plessis, the father of the Charismatic movement, said that G-d had showed him that after Israel became a nation, the Charismatic movement would begin. This is exactly what happened. G-d then began pouring out His Spirit on all flesh, just as the prophet Joel predicted thousands of years ago would happen in the last days!

The Six Day War in 1967 was also a very significant time in history. Jerusalem was brought back under Jewish rule for the first time since 70 A.D. Many Christians see this as the beginning of the fulfillment of Luke 21:24 which states that Jerusalem will be trodden down by the Gentiles until the times of the Gentiles are fulfilled.

I had the privilege of being born in 1948, the same year Israel was reborn and therefore was forty years old five days after Israel's fortieth birthday. In 1982 when I was praying and studying in Jerusalem during the Feast of Tabernacles, G-d lifted the veil from my eyes and I saw His purposes for Israel and how He is going to bring back the Jews from Russia, America and other nations. I also came to understand that the tremendous end-time revival mentioned in Ezekiel 37 is to happen in the land of Israel. I knew I would someday live in Jerusalem and spend time praying there and encouraging others to pray for Israel, for the return of the Jews to Israel, for the peace of Jerusalem, the redemption of the nations and the coming of the Messiah.

In honor of the rebirth of Israel, we sponsored "National Celebrations for Israel's Birthday" for four years in Washington, D.C., before moving to Israel, and honored various rabbis for building bridges with Christians. I had the privilege of being in Jerusalem and Israel more than twenty times before moving there in 1987. We have taken many groups of pastors and lay people, Jews and Christians, to tour the land, to celebrate the Feasts of the Lord and to pray for the peace of Jerusalem and the return of the Jews.

Many times we have prayed on the borders of Egypt, Jordan, Syria and Lebanon for the protection of Israel. Many times we have walked around the Old City praying for the peace of Jerusalem and peace between Jew and Arab, and the coming of the Messiah to bring everlasting peace. We have prayed for the Jewish people at synagogues. We have prayed for people in hospitals. We have met with soldiers at army bases and sang with them and given them gifts, prayed for them and blessed them. We even had the privilege of meeting the president and prime ministers of Israel.

I remember being in Jerusalem when the Ethiopian Jews first returned, and we prayed with them during their struggle to be integrated into Israeli society. We have taken hundreds of boxes of clothes to Israel for the Jewish people. We are planting a grove of trees called "SHALOM JERUSALEM GROVE" in Israel. Many of those on our tours have planted trees, not only in their names, but also in the names of their families and friends. Many have given their blood to the Jewish people. But we have all been blessed far more than we have blessed the Jewish people.

We have been blessed by the love of the Jewish people, and by the land they have restored. We have been blessed by the Bible, the Prophets, and the heritage we have in our Jewish roots. We have been blessed by the privilege of taking Jews and Christians to modern Israel, by all of our friends and guides in Israel, and by seeing many people come to know G-d in fuller ways by being in Israel. Seeing the Dead Sea scrolls and the fishing boat recently found in the Sea of Galilee from the time of Jesus blessed us greatly.

We have been blessed by all the beautiful biblical sites, and by falafels, vegetables for breakfast, and St. Peter's fish on the Sea of Galilee. We have been blessed by the beautiful Israeli music and dancing, children dancing at the Wall on *Simchat Torah*, and by the Sabbath rest when all businesses are closed. We have been blessed by observing Yom Kippur in the solemn silence of The Land as all activity ceases in remembrance of the blood atonement for our sins. The educational museums, the beautiful seas and the desert blossoming like a rose have blessed us as has the G-d of Israel, the G-d of Abraham, Isaac and Jacob.

Having been so privileged to witness these blessings, we feel a responsibility to help fulfill the Zionist vision. We have been so blessed by the land of Israel as Christians. One must wonder why the Jewish people, having been given their own nation back after the Holocaust, continue to sing the songs of Zion in the strange lands of Babylon instead of returning to their beautiful land of promise and destiny!

A great day is coming for the Jewish people who escape to Israel from the Gentile nations! In Ezekiel 39:28-29 G-d says He will gather them to their own land not leaving any behind. He will no longer hide His face from them for He will pour out His Spirit on the House of Israel.

If the first two returns brought such blessings on the world, how much more will this third return?

For the LORD will build up Zion and appear in his glory (Psalm 102:16)

The fullness of this third return will bring the coming of the Messiah.

The twentieth century truly has been a time of restoration. G-d began pouring out His Spirit on the Gentiles at the beginning of this century when, by His Spirit, He gave Theodore Herzl the vision of the restoration of Israel. This move of the Holy Spirit among both Jews and Christians has continued in increasing waves from the turn of the century until our time. The greatest day of restoration still is in the future as millions of Jews return from the Land of the North, America and other nations and as G-d pours out His Spirit upon the Jewish people in the land.

The first edition of this book was printed two days before the rioting began in Israel in December 1987. Many American Jews and Jews from other nations have been very critical of how the Israelis have handled the situation. Admittedly, they made mistakes. However, if the American Jews and others in "free" Western nations had followed G-d's call home to Israel over the fifty-five years since the rebirth of the nation, these problems would not exist as they do today! If the American Jews want to help the situation in Israel, they should stop pointing the finger and make *Aliyah*.

If the land of Israel was flourishing and overflowing with Jewish people, as the Prophets say it will be, the world would look on and say there is not even enough room for the Jews who just came through the Holocaust. But because the Jewish people have not returned from the West, only a fraction of the promised land is inhabited by the Jewish people while the remainder is considered "occupied territory" by world opinion—a territory belonging to others. If the American and Russian Jews had returned and begun possessing the land G-d had given them, then these problems would not have arisen. May they return soon before more problems arise.

David Ben Gurion said that by developing the Negev, Israel could be a country with a population the size of Belgium, according to Gershon Rivlin, an expert on Ben Gurion. Belgium, geographically the size of Israel, had ten million people when he made the statement. As of 1997, it has approximately six million.

I will surely gather all of you, O Jacob; I will surely bring together the remnant of Israel. I will bring them together like sheep in a pen, like a flock in its pasture; the place will throng with people. One who breaks open the way will go up before them; they will break through the gate and go out (Micah 2:12-13).

In 1987 Israel still had less than five million of the ten million people Ben Gurion envisioned in The Land. Room still remains for millions to return. In 2004 Israel's population has grown to almost seven million and there is vision and plans to settle one million Jews in the Negev as Ben Gurion saw.

Our concern is for those Jews in America who refuse to return to

Israel. While G-d says He will not leave any behind (Ezekiel 39:28-29), He never says they will *all* return, but that all of a *remnant* will return. According to this scripture, it seems that the Jewish people will either return to the land or die in the Diaspora.

As increasing judgements come on the Gentile nations, especially America, millions could be killed there unless they return soon. There are more than seven hundred scriptures (see Appendix A) calling the Jewish people to return to Israel, and I have yet to find *any* scriptures that specifically tell the Jewish people to remain in the Diaspora!

The second paragraph of the Sh'ma says:

And if you will obey my *mitzvoth* which I command you this day, to love *Adonai*, your G-d, and to serve Him with all your heart and with all your soul, He will give the rain for YOUR LAND in its season...Take heed lest...you perish quickly off THE GOOD LAND which *Adonai* gives you. You shall therefore lay up these words of Mine in your heart....And you shall write them upon the doorposts of your house and upon your gates, that your days and the days of your children may be multiplied IN THE LAND which *Adonai* swore to your fathers to give them, as long as the heavens are above the earth (see Deuteronomy 11:13-21).

In the words of Dr. David Stern: "The Sh'ma is not just for *mezuzot* on doorposts and gates in New York, Philadelphia, Washington and Los Angeles. It is a ringing encouragement to move on to *Eretz Yisrael*. Put your *mezuzah* on a doorpost in Jerusalem, Tel-Aviv, Haifa, Beersheva or Ariel! Return from exile *to the Land which G-d gave to your fathers* . . . and to you! Plan your *ALIYAH now!*"

Jewish people, escape to Israel before increasing judgements come on America. After thousands of years of persecution, it has been a blessing to hide under the security blanket of American society—but the blanket is being pulled off. G-d has never allowed you to be a completely assimilated people. G-d wants to regather you again from America. American Jews: Don't miss your destiny . . . discern the times in which you live! Return to

Israel and participate in the physical and spiritual restoration of all things in Israel.

Although Israel will also go through many difficult days in the future, her greatest days are still to come, days of greater glory than in King David's time, days that will bring the latter rain of the Holy Spirit that will be greater than the early rain. The days are approaching that will bring the coming of the Messiah! Obey the commandments of your G-d and return to Israel soon to participate in the natural and spiritual restoration of your promised land, your everlasting possession in the G-d of Israel!

5

Soviet Jews: Bound by Communism

Do not be afraid, for I am with you; I will bring your children from the east and gather you from the west. I will say to the north, "Give them up!" and to the south, "Do not hold them back." Bring my sons from afar and my daughters from the ends of the earth--everyone who is called by my name, whom I created for my glory, whom I formed and made.

All the nations gather together and the peoples assemble. Which of them foretold this and proclaimed to us the former things? Let them bring in their witnesses to prove they were right, so that others may hear and say, "It is true." "You are my witnesses," declares the LORD, "and my servant whom I have chosen, so that you may know and believe me and understand that I am he. Before me no G-d was formed, nor will there be one after me. I, even I, am the LORD, and apart from me there is no savior. I have revealed and saved and proclaimed--I, and not some foreign G-d among you. You are my witnesses," declares the LORD, "that I am G-d" (Isaiah 43:5-7, 9-12).

Forget the former things; do not dwell on the past. See, I am doing a new thing! Now it springs up; do you not perceive it? I am making a way in the desert and streams in the wasteland (Isaiah 43:18-19).

"However, the days are coming," declares the LORD, "when men will no longer say, 'As surely as the LORD lives, who brought the Israelites up out of Egypt,' but they will say, 'As surely as the LORD lives who brought the Israelites up out of the *land of the north*, and out of

**all the countries where he had banished them.' For I
will restore them to the land I gave their forefathers"
(Jeremiah 16:14-15).**

Almighty G-d is doing a new thing that may make the former Exodus out of Egypt look insignificant! The Pharaoh of the former Soviet Union is being forced to give up millions of Jewish people to return to Israel when G-d says to the North, "Give them up!" This has begun to happen after this book was written in 1987. In the last twenty years, over one million have already come home from the North!

In 1982, I had the privilege of meeting in Jerusalem with Steve Lightle and seven other people from different parts of Europe who had visions and were preparing for the exodus of the Jews from Russia. (Steve Lightle has written a book on the exodus of the Jews out of the USSR, called *Exodus II.) Ever* since that day, it was evident G-d was planning to bring the Jewish people out of the Soviet Union soon. *Exodus II* was going to become a reality and the burden of their deliverance became mine also.

In October of 1985, we led a prayer team of Jews and Christians to Egypt and Israel. On the top of Mount Sinai, where Moses prayed and G-d gave the vision to deliver the Jewish people out of Egypt, we prayed and called the Jews back to Israel. The prophetic message received at that time was: "You are reliving the Exodus of the past. Now I am calling you to go to Russia and America to prepare the way for the Exodus of the future!"

That message inspired our first Prayer Team to tour Russia in October of 1986. It was a major undertaking. Thirty-eight people went, both Jew and Christian. Visas were not granted to us by the Soviet Embassy in Washington, D.C., until eighteen hours before we departed and only after much intercessory prayer. G-d's presence and Holy Spirit greatly encompassed us on this prayer tour. One church had 24-hour daily prayer watches during the whole trip. Dozens of churches and hundreds of individuals also prayed fervently.

We arrived at Leningrad on a cold night. It was raining and hailing. As soon as we got off the plane and onto the bus, KGB guards abruptly faced us with a cold chilling stare and silently seemed to be saying, "We welcome you to this no-nonsense, humanistic, atheistic country!"

First, we visited the Hermitage Museum in Leningrad, one of the best art museums in the world. Ironically, it was filled with Jewish and Christian art from the seventeenth to the nineteenth centuries. Then, we met with a number of different Refuseniks (Jews who had lost their jobs because of applying for emigration to Israel). They shared with us how they were being mistreated and persecuted because of their desire to return to Israel. They were very grateful for our prayers, encouragement and gifts. They all have subsequently been released to return to Israel.

I spent most of a night with Valeri Barinov, a Christian musician in Leningrad, who has led hundreds, perhaps thousands, of Gentiles to the Lord in Leningrad. (Not only Jews, but also Christians were being persecuted in the USSR!) Every year the Soviets moved him from one job to another because he led so many to know G-d, including KGB agents. He was eventually put in jail for three years, where he was badly persecuted, including having his ribs broken for talking about G-d—but this did not stop him. He probably led a hundred people to the Lord in prison, where he started a church. The KGB was so frustrated that they released him from prison a few weeks before we met him. He is the most fearless person I have ever met. He released the Trumpet Call to the world and has been written up in *Rolling Stone* magazine and other publications.

On *Yom Kippur*, we visited the Synagogue in Moscow and gave clothing and Bibles to the Jewish people. We also did a Jericho march around the Kremlin and Red Square, like Joshua did around Jericho, praying for the release of the Jews. We were told later that the Jews are in one prison that is literally under the Kremlin.

We also sang, "O Come Let Us Adore Him," in front of KGB agents in a museum that was once the Church of the Annunciation. There were beautiful pictures of Jesus' birth in this museum right in the heart of the Kremlin. Our time in the Soviet Union was during the three days of the Summit meeting with President Reagan and Secretary General Gorbachov in Iceland. This opened up many doors of conversation through which many lives were eternally changed.

Progressing directly from Moscow to Jerusalem, we helped prepare "The Highway of Deliverance," by praying through Europe on our way back to the promised land. From the Free Russian Church on the Mount of Olives in Jerusalem, we commanded the North, in the name of the G-d of Israel, to give up the Jews (Isaiah 43:6), and we called them back to Israel. Within a few days after this prayer mission to Russia the Communists agreed to release 12,000 Jews to Israel within a year!

Our second prayer tour to Russia took place in March and April of 1987, just a few days after my traumatic vision related in the first chapter. After this vision of bombs going off over my head and America being attacked by the forces of Islam, we left on this mission knowing we were on a divine call. In Moscow, G-d opened the book of Daniel and Revelation to us. Daniel 10 shows how the archangel Michael helped Daniel understand G-d's plan for the Jewish people at the end of the age. G-d showed us from Daniel 12:1 that Michael was arising to deliver the Jewish people out of the Soviet Union.

A remarkable "coincidence" is that one of the major church museums in the Kremlin is called "The Church of Michael the Archangel," who is the angel traditionally associated with the protection of the Jews. We prayed in the church for the Jews' deliverance and enjoyed the beautiful biblical art! We also saw that as Michael the Archangel arose, that he would take on Lucifer as mentioned in Revelation 12:6-8 and that there would be war in heaven and Lucifer would be cast out of the second heaven upon the earth, embody the false Messiah and a great war would be manifested in the earth, beginning the Great Tribulation.

Sensing that it was time for Michael the Archangel to arise and for the Jews to be released as Daniel 12:1 states, we did another Jericho March around the Kremlin. We prayed, asking G-d to release Michael and the other angels under him to arise and deliver the Jews back to Israel from both the USSR and other countries.

We also visited the Atheistic Museum in Leningrad. This building was an old church building that was converted into a museum. The bottom floor consisted of an extremely large statue of a nude man, representing the G-d of humanistic Communism, with little cherubs or devils around him. The central focus was a picture of Lenin with all the religions and cultures of the world being subjugated by Communism. The American, British, Swiss and other flags were torn in half and the hammer and sickle triumphed over the world. We did another Jericho March around the Atheistic Museum, and with the Sword of the Spirit laid the ax to the spiritual root of Communism in the very city where Lenin instituted this demonic ideology in 1917. (It is interesting to note that 1987 was the seventieth anniversary of the Communist Revolution!) Praise G-d this Atheistic Museum closed three years later.

As of this writing, the Refuseniks with whom people in our prayer tour met have been released, including Vladmir Slepak, Mikhail Zivin and Helen May who since translated this book into Russian in Jerusalem. Margaret Thatcher was very instrumental in the release of Valeri Barinov who, along with his family, spent a day praying with us at our House of Prayer in Jerusalem in early 1988.

G-d has increasingly brought plagues on humanistic, atheistic Communism, and millions of Soviet Jews are to be set free. Shabtai Alboher said in the *Jerusalem Post*, "Soviet Jewish activists, unencumbered by the culture and distorted values of the American exile today have truly expressed the authentic Jewish spirit much more than the American Jews." Over the past fifty years, fifty times as many Soviet Jews per million population made *Aliyah* than did American Jews.

While I believe strongly in the continuing Exodus of the Jews from the North and have been working towards that end, I concur with Anatoly (now Natan) Scharansky, a leading Soviet Refusenik and current minister in Israel's government. During his visit to Washington, D.C., a few months after he was released from prison in Russia to make *Aliyah* to Israel, Scharansky said, "The enemies in the USA are much more subtle, deceptive and difficult to recognize."

The G-d of materialism in the USA has a stronger hold on the Jewish people than the G-d of atheism had in the USSR. G-d says He wants to bring the Jews out of not only the Land of the North, but all nations. This means His biggest task is getting them back from the USA to Israel. Many believe the Exodus from Russia and America will be more spectacular than out of Egypt. If necessary, G-d will bring plagues and judgements not only on the Pharaoh of atheistic Communism in Russia, but also on the G-d of materialism in the Babylon of America to "GIVE UP" the Jewish people!

More of the Jews coming out of the Land of the North to go to Israel end up being seduced by the G-d of mammon and coming to America instead. Even though fifty times as many Jews from the North went to Israel than American Jews from 1987 to 2001, the *Jerusalem Post* reported that in 1987 some eighty percent of the Soviet Jews that were given exit visas to Israel so far that year went to America.

Unless American Jews set an example by breaking free from materialism in following the commandments of G-d to make *Aliyah* to Israel and become practicing Zionists, the Soviet Jews will continue to follow the G-d of materialism and luxury to America rather than following their call, deliverance and destiny to Zion! (Since the writing of this book, a law in America limiting the number of Jewish people coming into America is the main reason most are going to Israel, although many still go to the USA.)

6

New York and America – the Heart of Babylon

By the rivers of Babylon, there we sat down, yea, we wept, when we remembered Zion. We hanged our harps upon the willows in the midst thereof. For there they that carried us away captive required of us a song; and they that wasted us required of us mirth, saying, Sing us one of the songs of Zion. How shall we sing the LORD'S song in a strange land? If I forget thee, O Jerusalem, let my right hand forget her cunning. If I do not remember thee, let my tongue cleave to the roof of my mouth; if I prefer not Jerusalem above my chief joy.

Remember, O LORD, the children of Edom in the day of Jerusalem; who said, Rase it, rase it, even to the foundation thereof. O Daughter of Babylon, who art to be destroyed; happy shall he be, that rewardeth thee as thou hast served us. Happy shall he be, that taketh and dasheth thy little ones against the stones (Psalm 137 KJV).

Come out of her, my people! Run for your lives! Run from the fierce anger of the LORD...You who have escaped the sword, leave and do not linger! Remember the LORD in a distant land, and think on Jerusalem (Jeremiah 51:45, 50).

Just as in ancient times when the Israelites wept by the rivers of Babylon and promised never to forget Jerusalem, so today the Jewish people are sitting by a river of Babylon in America. The difference is that they are not yet weeping to return to Jerusalem.

Ezekiel 17:1-10 is an allegory about *two great eagles*. The first eagle depicts ancient Babylon and, though the second eagle historically was Egypt, it is also applicable to the end-time Daughter of Babylon, whom is believed by some to be New York and America. Ezekiel tells how the first eagle, the King of Babylon, came to Jerusalem and took King Jehoiachin captive. Daniel and thousands of others of the Jewish people were physically taken captive to Babylon by Nebuchadnezzar. Second Kings 24 says that all were taken except the poorest people.

The Jews were greatly blessed during their seventy years in Babylonian captivity and accumulated great wealth. Ezekiel tells how the vine of Israel grew and became a spreading vine of low stature, *whose branches turned toward this eagle alone, and the vine prospered*. Then:

> **But there was another great eagle with large wings and many feathers; and behold, this vine bent its roots toward him, and stretched its branches toward him, from the garden terrace where it had been planted, that he might water it. It was planted in good soil by many waters, to bring forth branches, bear fruit, and become a majestic vine.**

> **Say, "Thus says the Lord G-d: 'Will it thrive? Will he not pull up its roots, cut off its fruit, and leave it to wither? All of its spring leaves will wither, and no great power or many people will be needed to pluck it up by its roots. Behold, it is planted, will it thrive? Will it not utterly wither when the *east wind* touches it? It will wither in the garden terrace where it grew'" (Ezekiel 17:7-10 NKJV).**

An east wind is a definite sovereign act of Almighty G-d. Ezekiel 19:12 gives another example of an east wind:

> **But it was uprooted in fury and thrown to the ground. The east wind made it shrivel, it was stripped of its fruit; its strong branches withered and fire consumed them (Ezekiel 19:12).**

These insights are partially taken from the writings of Dr. Robert

Hooley, former pastor of Faith Bible Church in Denver, Colorado. G-d's purpose is for His people to return to Israel; but those who refuse could be caught in the fire of a nuclear holocaust! Yet, it is worth mentioning, more Jewish people left Israel for America than came to Israel from America in 1987 and in many other years.

The assimilation of Jewish people into Gentile culture and the number joining religious cults are just a few of the judgements of the east wind that are already affecting the future of the Jewish community in America. Although they have not yet caused substantial Jewish emigration to Jerusalem, other judgements are coming very soon which will cause the Jewish people to weep and many to return to Israel from the USA.

The historic city of Babylon was famous for its wealth and hedonism. The center of life was focused around man, his rights, his pleasures, his ease and wealth and comfort. The book of Revelation chapters 17 and 18 describe Babylon in the last days in a similar manner. Babylon is described as a literal, geographic city, although it also seems to be a world-wide system and in a broader sense, consists of the evil cities of the world.

The two characteristics that most exemplify Babylon in Revelation are materialism and hedonism. New York is not only the leading city in the world regarding money and materialism (with the World Money Market centered there), but also may be the leading city in the world regarding perversion and hedonism.

New York and America are the heart of Babylon today. New York and America have become a man-centered society. We are referred to as the "me" generation; man, self, materialism, hedonism, ease and luxury are worshiped rather than the true G-d of Israel (just as in Babylon of old). We have spent hundreds of hours praying for New York City, praying that revival and blessing come to the City, and that the Jews leave before destruction comes.

Revelation 18:3 says that "the kings of the earth committed adultery with [Babylon], and the merchants of the earth grew rich from her excessive luxuries." G-d gave her torture and grief for the equivalency of luxury and glory she gave herself. "In her heart she boasts, 'I sit as a queen; I am not a widow, and I will never mourn'" (verse 7). Some believe the Fourth of July celebration in New York in 1986, with all the drunkenness, materialism, sensuality and boasting in "The Queen" (the Statue of Liberty), exemplified Babylon moving toward the fullness of her cup and becoming ripe for judgement.

We live as if the rest of the world and its troubles cannot affect us, but Revelation 18:8-10 says: "In one day her plagues will overtake her: death, mourning and famine. She will be consumed by fire, for mighty is the Lord G-d who judges her! When the kings of the earth who committed adultery with her and shared her luxury see the smoke of her burning, they will weep and mourn over her. Terrified at her torment, they will stand far off and cry: 'Woe! Woe, O great city, O Babylon, city of power! In one hour your doom has come!'" This judgement on Babylon (New York) and America will come soon.

The United Nations is centered in New York. The nations within the United Nations have allowed the killing of more than 100 million of their own citizens by various means. This has happened through oppressive regimes in countries such as Russia, China, Cuba and others. In addition, approximately one billion abortions have been performed worldwide. Man formed the United Nations to try to bring together the nations of the world, but this has not succeeded. The United Nations has generally proven to be very anti-Israel over the past fifty-five years, despite the fact that the UN officially recognized Israel's existence and received it as a member in 1948.

When we led a prayer team in New York to pray at the United Nations, we saw the sign that has the famous scripture from Isaiah 2 on it which reads:

They shall beat their swords into plowshares, and their spears into pruning hooks; nation shall not lift up sword against nation, neither shall they learn war any more (Isaiah 2:4 KJV).

This is a noble banner with a noble aim, but G-d's plan shows that world peace will proceed from *Jerusalem,* not New York. Isaiah 2:3 (KJV) states:

For out of Zion shall go forth the Law, and the word of the LORD from Jerusalem.

G-d will judge between the nations and settle disputes for many peoples. Isaiah 11 also says that Israel is a banner for the nations, not New York! Unity, world redemption and restoration of the people of G-d are not going to spring from New York (Babylon), but from Jerusalem (Psalm 48:2). Also, the Messiah is not coming to New York, but as Zechariah 14 says, He will come to Jerusalem and stand upon the Mount of Olives.

Why are there more Jews in New York than any city in the world and more Jews in America than any nation in the world? Despite a Holocaust that killed six million Jewish people in a foreign land, and despite the rebirth of their homeland, Israel, just fifty-five years ago, they refuse to leave America. Historically, as today, they found it easier and more comfortable to live in Babylon than to rebuild in a war-torn land. Today they are more committed to materialism and ease in Babylon and being an American Jew than G-d's call for them to return to their end time destiny in the land of Israel. Secular and *Torah*-based Jewish people alike in America are not taking seriously some seven hundred scriptures calling the Jewish people to escape the Babylon of America and other nations and return to the land of Israel.

Shabtai Alboher said in the *Jerusalem Post*:

"When former prisoner of Zion Yosef Mendelevich was caught trying to hijack a plane from Leningrad to Israel, the Soviets offered him a choice: death, or life on the condition that he renounce his Zionism and allegiance to the Jewish state. In prison, they tried to persuade him by convincing him that he was really a Russian at heart. 'You're one of us,' they told him, 'We speak the same language, grew up together, shared the same experiences. What makes you think you're any different from us?' At this point Mendelevich realized that the greatest threat to his life and freedom was not imprisonment, but the possibility of denying his Jewish identity. He asked himself a question that most American Jews will not yet consider posing: 'Would my life have value if I cannot be myself? That is, if I can't express my Jewishness!' Mendelevich refused to recant and today lives as a free man in Jerusalem."

The Jewish people in America, other nations, and even some in Israel seem to have in many ways lost their true sense of purpose, uniqueness, identity and destiny as a people. Their Jewish national identity falls victim to the lure of luxury in the US. Their values are such that they prefer a Mercedes in America to a modest apartment in Jerusalem. They seem to have forgotten their high calling to be the head and not the tail among the nations.

Many religious and nonreligious Jewish people in America, and even some in Israel, have been seduced by (and find themselves trying to emulate) the secular materialist priorities of the Babylon of America rather than fulfilling their destiny in G-d by leading the way in righteousness in Israel as a light to the nations. This is exemplified by the fact that over the last fifty-five years, over three hundred thousand Jews have left Israel for America, while approximately eighty thousand have made *Aliyah* to Israel from America.

It seems that the only things that will cause massive *Aliyah* movements from America are judgement or spiritual revival. Increased anti-Semitism in America, an economic crash, and other judgements on America could spur *Aliyah*. (This manuscript was originally prepared before "Black Monday" of October, 1987, when the stock market fell 508 points.)

A preferable means would be for biblically based revival movements, such as the "*teshuvah*" of the 1960s, to break out within all branches of Judaism. When the Jewish people begin to respond to their biblical call as Israelites to make *Aliyah* and to love their G-d and Zion, they will turn from serving the G-ds of materialism and luxury in Babylon as "American" Jews. Hopefully, it will be revival, not judgement that will bring the American Jews home to Israel. Psalm 137:8, listed at the beginning of this chapter, says the Daughter of Babylon is to be destroyed. I believe G-d is speaking in Revelation 18:4 (KJV) to the Jewish people in New York and America:

Come out of her [Babylon—USA] my people so that you will not share in her sins, so you will not receive any of her plagues.

Zechariah 2:7 (KJV) says: "Deliver thyself, O Zion, that dwellest with the Daughters of Babylon." G-d is beckoning and calling the Jews home to Israel. Will they respond to G-d's wooing, begin weeping for Jerusalem again, and return to Israel—or be caught in a devastating tragedy like the Holocaust?

7

American Jews: Bound by Materialism

Those who cling to worthless idols forfeit the grace that could be theirs (Jonah 2:8).

Shake off your dust; rise up, sit enthroned, O Jerusalem. Free yourself from the chains on your neck, O captive Daughter of Zion. For this is what the LORD says: "You were sold for nothing, and without money you will be redeemed" (Isaiah 52:2-3).

Arise, shine, for your light has come, and the glory of the LORD rises upon you. See, darkness covers the earth and thick darkness is over the peoples, but the LORD rises upon you and his glory appears over you. Nations will come to your light, and kings to the brightness of your dawn.

Lift up your eyes and look about you: All assemble and come to you; your sons come from afar, and your daughters are carried on the arm. Then you will look and be radiant, your heart will throb and swell with joy; the wealth on the seas will be brought to you, to you the riches of the nations will come. Herds of camels will cover your land, young camels of Midian and Ephah. And all from Sheba will come, bearing gold and incense and proclaiming the praise of the LORD. All Kedar's flocks will be gathered to you, the rams of Nebaioth will serve you; they will be accepted as offerings on my altar, and I will adorn my glorious temple.

Who are these that fly along like clouds, like doves to their nests? Surely the islands look to me; in the lead

are the ships of Tarshish, bringing your sons from afar, with their silver and gold, to the honor of the LORD your G-d, the Holy One of Israel, for he has endowed you with splendor.

Foreigners will rebuild your walls, and their kings will serve you. Though in anger I struck you, in favor I will show you compassion. Your gates will always stand open, they will never be shut, day or night, so that men may bring you the wealth of the nations--their kings led in triumphal procession. For the nation or kingdom that will not serve you will perish; it will be utterly ruined.

The glory of Lebanon will come to you, the pine, the fir and the cypress together, to adorn the place of my sanctuary; and I will glorify the place of my feet. The sons of your oppressors will come bowing before you; all who despise you will bow down at your feet and will call you the City of the LORD, Zion of the Holy One of Israel (Isaiah 60:1-14).

The wealth of all the surrounding nations will be collected--great quantities of gold and silver and clothing. (Zechariah 14:14).

I t is time for the Jewish people in America to set an example for the Russian Jews. It is time to break from the G-d of materialism in America and to take whatever wealth they have in America back to Israel as they did from Egypt and Babylon centuries ago!

The stereotype of "rich American Jews" is a misconception. Most are average in income. In 1986, eight hundred thousand Jews in the USA were living below the poverty level. However, the Jewish people in America are still just as bound emotionally and economically as the Jewish people in Russia were bound physically in their country. Historically, the Jewish people in Egypt were physically bound under slavery and could not prosper, while in Babylon they prospered and were bound under the influence of materialism. Today secularism is being manifested through the face of materialism in America. As many of them throughout history did not want to leave the Diaspora when G-d told them to, the same is true in America today.

Shabtai Alboher, a Jewish lawyer from New York who recently made *Aliyah,* asks in a *Jerusalem Post* article:

> Why are Jewish activists not protesting at the United States Embassy in Tel Aviv demanding, 'LET MY PEOPLE GO!'? Everyone assumes, of course, that American Jews are free to join their brethren in the Jewish state. But, in reality, American Jews are acting like an oppressed nation that has subordinated its national identity, perhaps unwittingly, to an adopted society and culture.

> Despite their physical freedom, American Jews have become enslaved intellectually, emotionally and economically to a materialistic consumer culture that worships dollars and idolizes individual gain and material gratification.

> As thousands of Soviet Jews have risked economic hardship, torture, and "Siberian vacations" to touch the cherished soil of Israel, American Jews, shackled to their freedom, dial their stockbrokers and plan to exit to kosher Caribbean resorts.

> Out of a Jewish community about one-third the size of that in the US, approximately one million Jews have immigrated to Israel from the former USSR nations since 1948, compared to only about eighty thousand from the "land of the free," the USA [numbers adjusted as of 2003].

Many believe that Israel could not exist without Jewish philanthropic support. American and other Jews use this argument to justify not making *Aliyah,* but this is not true. In an article entitled, "Give Us People, Not Cash" in the *Jerusalem Post*, dated December 5, 1987, Shlomo Anineri says:

> Let us seriously consider emancipating Israel from direct financial dependence on Jewish philanthropy. The United Jewish Appeal and its affiliates should be abolished.

All worldwide Jewish Fund Raising amounts on an annual basis to about two percent of Israel's budget...It is obvious that the Israeli leaders, who mainly address Jewish audiences abroad on fund-raising occasions, find it intrinsically difficult to tackle the quest of *Aliyah* at the same time.

Israel does not need overseas Jewish philanthropy for its survival. No, it needs the Jewish people in the Diaspora to come home [make *Aliyah*] with whatever money they may have to Israel, their promised land.

Materialism is not the only issue. The Jewish people have been so persecuted for thousands of years that many no longer want to face their Jewishness. They need their faith rebuilt to return to Israel. May G-d give them strength, faith, courage and hope to resettle one last time before their Messiah comes.

Anatoly Scharansky, a man of great faith, said in Washington, D.C.:

I believe it would be more difficult to live in America than the Soviet Union, because in Russia you know who your enemy is; consequently, you can deal with him; but in the United States, there are so many subtle enemies which could disguise themselves as your friends, such as materialism (mammon), sensuality, pride, the cares of this world, etc., that it's more difficult to know who and what you are fighting.

There are so many choices to make in America, things can consequently be more complex and difficult. It is obviously more difficult to break from the materialistic culture of America than to break from Russia and return to Israel. Looking at percentages, only one American Jew made *Aliyah* to every fifty Soviet Jews over the last fifty-five years.

We increasingly realize the degree of bondage the Jewish people and Christians in America have to the G-d of materialism. We print on our money, "In G-d We Trust," but it seems that the G-d we trust in is the very money on which we are printing "In G-d We Trust." The exposure of the

G-d of mammon seducing Christian ministries in America in 1987 is only an extreme case of how many others of us as Christians and Jews have been seduced to lesser degrees.

We have to struggle personally to make decisions based on obeying G-d and doing the things He is calling us to do, while resisting the temptation of doing the accepted thing that would appear to be more financially beneficial. I Timothy 6:10 says that the love of money is the root of all kinds of evil, Matthew 6:24 says: **"No one can serve two masters. Either he will hate the one and love the other, or he will be devoted to the one and despise the other. You cannot serve G-d and mammon."**

Many in the Jewish and Christian communities have been deceived and seduced by these false G-ds. We have not taken the Second Commandment seriously which states:

Thou shalt have no other G-ds before me (Exodus 20:3 KJV).

We have not discerned the false G-ds of our contemporary culture: greed, sexual perversion, sensuality and selfishness, which are all manifestations of materialism. Consequently, we have not been able to see the forest from the trees. The abortionists, drug pushers, pimps and prostitutes, corporate executives, sports heroes, Hollywood and rock star heroes, common laborers who are trying to "keep up with the Joneses," nominal and religious Christians and Jews alike, have been bound by materialism in many different forms.

Before warning Nineveh of coming judgement, Jonah came to a crucial realization in the belly of the fish:

Those who cling to worthless idols forfeit the grace that could be theirs (Jonah 2:8).

According to the August 27, 1987, issue of the *Jerusalem Post*, one thousand Jews a month were leaving what was then the Soviet Union. Only ten percent of the more secular Jews leaving are going to Israel, while nearly one hundred percent of the *Torah*-based religious Jews are returning to Israel. However, the G-d of materialism in America is so strong, it even blinds and stops the *Torah*-based orthodox and other religious Jews, including Messianic Jews, in America from following the over seven hundred scriptures calling them back to the Land (see Appendix A). May the scriptures and the example of the religious Russian Jews who have made *Aliyah* provoke religious American Jews to follow the *Torah* in making *Aliyah*.

Unless the G-d of mammon in America can be cast out of the Church and the Jewish people through prayer, G-d will move to bring down Wall Street and materialism in America: He is a jealous G-d and will have no other G-ds before Him. (This conclusion was drawn in September 1987, before "Black Monday" shook many people's confidence.)

In 1857, within a few weeks after Wall Street fell, the greatest prayer revival in American history began in New York led by Jeremiah Lanpheir, and spread across America. Churches were filled throughout New York and America to pray every noon. In some towns, businesses even shut down to pray! G-d may cause our economy to fall so that people might again cry out to the true G-d of Israel.

It is time for the Jews to escape the Daughter of Babylon before it's too late. Today is the day of deliverance for the Jewish people. Today you can return to Israel and take your finances with you. As Isaiah 60 says, the wealth of the nations should be taken back to Israel! If Isaiah 60 is speaking to anyone today, it is primarily to the Jewish people in America, not the Soviet Union. America is where two-thirds of the Jews in the Diaspora live, and where most of the money is!

If the Jewish people don't follow G-d's call to the land of Israel, when Wall Street and our economy falls completely, the Jews could become a scapegoat, as they have many times in history. They were blamed during the Black Death in Europe, one of the worst plagues in history. During the Dreyfus case in France (the homeland of liberty and the great revolution), a Jewish army officer was falsely accused of selling military secrets to Germany. The Jews were targeted in the pogroms (massacres) in Russia in the 1800s before the revolution. Today the Jewish people are falsely accused in many countries. In the Middle East, Israel is the scapegoat for many problems that arise there.

When Wall Street and the American economy falls, the Jews could once again be falsely accused. The director of the Federal Reserve for the past two decades, Alan Greenspan, is Jewish and said he believed there would be a recession. The fall of Wall Street or a depression of our economy could spark increased anti-Semitism throughout America, as happened with Father McLaughlin during the "Great Depression" of the 1930s.

G-d wants the Jewish people to go to Israel with their money just as they came out of Egypt to Israel. He wants them to take whatever riches they have in the nations back to Israel before the Stock Market and economy collapses in America. Today is the day of full deliverance. If they wait much longer, because of the coming judgements on America, they will probably go back with nothing, if they are able to return at all! Investing in Jerusalem today could prove to be the best investment in the world.

On November 2, 1987, G-d gave to the Venezuelan pastor, Jaime Puertas, a vision in Jerusalem showing him that the United States of America is preparing a law that will forbid money to be taken out of America in large amounts. The Jews who believe in the prophecy will hurry to sell their possessions, before the law is enacted. They will return, bringing the riches of the nations (Isaiah 60:5), and full of blessings, like the fat cows that Pharaoh dreamed about (see Genesis 41). But, because of their unbelief, those who will not believe will return with empty sacks and mourning, like the lean, ugly cows.

The kind of law that Jaime Puertas saw in his vision is already in force in Latin America and Spain, and will be adopted by other nations. (Pastor Puertas has started two thousand congregations in Spanish-speaking countries. He had just completed a forty-day fast along with a hundred and twenty others from his congregations for the "Return of the Captives of Zion to Israel" when he received the vision).

May the American Jews not repeat the tragedy of the history of the Jewish State. Approximately ninety percent of those who have returned have waited until they were refugees—the poor, lame, halt and blind from the nations. May Wall Street "LET MY PEOPLE GO!" May G-d execute His judgements on the G-d of materialism. May the Jewish people break from materialism in America and come home to Israel before it's too late!

Isaiah 60:5 says the wealth of the seas and the riches of the nations will be brought to Israel. Not only are the Jewish people to take themselves and their money back to Israel, but this verse says others will bring the riches of the nations to Israel as well. May G-d give the Jewish people favor in America as He did in Egypt so that Americans will give them money to bless Israel.

> **Now the LORD had said to Moses, "I will bring one more plague on Pharaoh and on Egypt. After that, he will let you go from here, and when he does, he will drive you out completely. Tell the people that men and women alike are to ask their neighbors for articles of silver and gold" (Exodus 11:1-2).**

May G-d lift the veil from the eyes of Christians and increasingly lead them to help the Jewish people fulfill this scripture by also investing their money in Israel and encouraging others to do the same.

Precious Jewish people, it's time to stop saying, "I'm an American Jew." Stop bowing down and worshiping the G-d of materialism in America, and fulfill your end-time biblical destiny. Return to the land of your forefathers to worship the G-d of Abraham, Isaac and Jacob with all your heart!

Jewish and Christian Zionism

The LORD had said to Abram, "Leave your country, your people and your father's household and go to the land I will show you. I will make you into a great nation and I will bless you; I will make your name great, and you will be a blessing. I will bless those who bless you, and whoever curses you I will curse; and all peoples on earth will be blessed through you" (Genesis 12:1-3).

The LORD will have compassion on Jacob; once again he will choose Israel and will settle them in their own land. Aliens will join them and unite with the house of Jacob. Nations will take them and bring them to their own place. And the house of Israel will possess the nations as menservants and maidservants in the LORD'S land (Isaiah 14:1-2).

"And foreigners who bind themselves to the LORD to serve him, to love the name of the LORD, and to worship him, all who keep the Sabbath without desecrating it and who hold fast to my covenant--these I will bring to my holy mountain and give them joy in my house of prayer. Their burnt offerings and sacrifices will be accepted on my altar; for my house will be called a house of prayer for all nations." The Sovereign LORD declares--he who gathers the exiles of Israel: "I will gather still others to them besides those already gathered" (Isaiah 56:6-8).

G-d has continually been joining Jewish people and Christians together to pray and work for the rebirth and restoration of Israel and the third return of the Jewish people to their promised land for almost four hundred years. Zionism has its roots with Abraham who first emigrated to Jerusalem four thousand years ago. Abraham was neither a Jew nor a Christian but a man who followed G-d, going out not knowing where he was going. Abraham was looking for the heavenly Jerusalem whose builder and maker is G-d, when G-d led him to discover the earthly Jerusalem. He is the Father of all Jewish and Christian Zionists.

There have been millions of natural Zionists since that time who have made *Aliyah* and lived and worked as practical Zionists in the Land of Israel, and millions of others who have helped from afar in the Diaspora. There have also been hundreds of millions of spiritual Zionists, many who have not understood G-d's purposes for natural Zion.

Biblically, a true Jewish or Christian Zionist believes in both a natural and spiritual Zion as did King David. A Zionist biblically is someone who is seeking and following G-d with all his heart as Abraham our father did. Anyone who does that will eventually come to understand both natural and spiritual Zion.

Zion has several meanings in the Bible. It refers first of all, to physical Zion, Mount Zion, the place where David brought the Ark of the Covenant in Jerusalem, as well as the City of Jerusalem and even the Land of Israel as a whole (Psalm 48:2; Psalm 137). Spiritually, Zion in the Old Testament and New Testament refers to the Presence of G-d.

King David believed in the heart of Zion as Jerusalem and Israel, but it wasn't until the Ark with G-d's Presence came to Zion that the natural and spiritual dimension of Zion became one. Biblically, there have been many Jewish Zionists, like Joshua and Caleb, who led the first return and Ezra, Nehemiah and Zerubbabel who led the second return. Ruth is a well-known example of a non-Jewish Zionist from biblical times, but there also were many others.

The term "modern-day Zionism" appeared first in 1890. Theodore Herzl is the father of modern-day Zionism. He wrote *The Jewish State* and called the first Zionist conference in Basel, Switzerland in 1897. But many Jewish and Christian Zionists worked together as precursors of this return to the Land by preparing the way for Herzl.

The following examples relate how Jewish and Christian Zionists worked together for the restoration of Israel and helped prepare the way for this third return of the Jewish people to the Land:

1200 A.D. – St. Francis of Assisi, who was going to fight in the Crusades, had a vision. G-d told him to leave the Crusades, give away his horse and all his belongings, and follow Jesus as a true Christian. He led a pilgrimage to Jerusalem at the beginning of the 13th century and started an Order. The Franciscans were the sole guardians of the Holy Places. The Franciscans, Duns Scotus and William of Occom, were known as forerunners of the Christian Zionists as early as the 13th century.

1609 – Despite the example of the Franciscans, the time of Christian Zionism did not really begin until 1609. It was then that Thomas Brightman, a Christian theologian known as the father of the "British Doctrine of Restoration of the Jews," wrote in *The Vision Was There*: "The Jews will go to Palestine and thus restore their kingdom. There is nothing more certain, the prophets everywhere confirm it."

1649 – Two English Puritans (Christians) of Amsterdam, Joanna and Ebenezer Cartwright, petitioned "That the nation of England with the inhabitants of the Netherlands shall be the first and readiest to transport Israel's sons and daughters on ships to the land of their forefathers, Abraham, Isaac and Jacob, their everlasting possession." This petition to the English government had two parts: (1) England is to assist in restoration of the people of Israel to the land of Palestine; and, (2) Lift the three hundred and fifty year ban of Jews in England.

1650 – Manasseh Ben Israel, a learned rabbi of Amsterdam, published a book called *The Hope of Israel* in 1650. What Manasseh had in mind was to open England to the Jews in order that the Diaspora would be truly world-wide. This was necessary before the ingathering of the exiles could begin.

1655 – Manasseh Ben Israel and three other rabbis travelled to London from Amsterdam (invited by Oliver Cromwell) and convinced the English Parliament to compromise and receive the Jewish people into England. Cromwell's interest in Manasseh Ben Israel was the stepping-stone to other joinings of Jewish and Christian Zionists to accomplish G-d's purposes in the restoration of Israel in the years to follow. In 1660, Jews were readmitted to England.

1727 – Count Zinzendorf and the Moravians started a community and 24-hour prayer which lasted for a hundred and twenty years in Herrnhut, Germany, for the restoration of Jerusalem and Israel based on Isaiah 62:6-7.

1840 – Lord Shaftesbury was said to be the purest man in Westminster. He may have done more for the poor than any man in government throughout history. Charles Dickens called his "10-Hour Bill" the finest piece of legislation ever enacted in England up to that time. Shaftesbury and many with him in the Great Awakening espoused the restoration of Israel as did the Puritans two hundred years before him.

In 1840, the *London Times* published Lord Shaftesbury's plan to plant the Jewish people in the land of their forefathers. He was successful in establishing an Anglican Bishopric in Jerusalem and an Anglican church on the shores of Palestine, according to *The Bible and the Sword* by Barbara Tuchman.

An Orthodox Jewish friend of Shaftesbury in England, Sir Moses Montefiore, believed, like him, in the literal restoration of the Jewish State and worked together with him towards this end. Montefiore and Shaftesbury were another example of Jewish and Christian Zionists who worked together before the rebirth of Israel. This was still at a time when the Jews themselves had not yet come to believe the idea of a Jewish State. It was another fifty-five years until Herzl wrote his book, *The Jewish State*.

1845 – Mordecai Manuel Noah published the *Discourse on the Restoration of the Jews* in the USA. It was the first attempt to bring the restoration doctrine into accord with Jewish concepts since Menasseh Ben Israel. Noah declared that the United States will pave the way for the restoration to Zion! He said, "Christian and Jew will, together on Mount Zion, raise their voices in praise of Him whose covenant with Abraham was to endure forever and in whose seed all the nations of the earth are to be blessed."

Noah had no hesitation in advocating a more candid union between

Christians and Jews. He declared, "Nothing in my opinion will save the nation from sinking into oblivion, but agitating this subject of restoration. We should pass the word around the world, 'Restoration of the Jews,' 'Justice to Israel,' 'The rights and independence of the Hebrews,' 'Restore them to their country,' 'Redeem them from captivity.' Christians should be involved to aid them in this good cause."

Mordecai Manuel Noah was a prophetic voice before his time. He was speaking to our generation. Today Jewish and Christian Zionists are cooperating to help in the return of the Jews and are raising their voices together in praise on Mount Zion.

1860 – Moses Hess was a Jewish leader who lived in Cologne, Germany, and was the editor of the Cologne newspaper. Karl Marx edited the same newspaper after Moses Hess. While Karl Marx, a Jew, moved from Cologne to London and wrote *Das Kapital*, the Communist manifesto, Moses Hess became a Zionist and wrote a book called *From Rome to Jerusalem* which was a forerunner of *The Jewish State* by Theodore Herzl.

When Theodore Herzl read the book by Moses Hess, he said in essence that Moses Hess was the first Zionist, but one generation before the appointed time. While in Berlin the Jewish leaders were seeking to establish a Jewish state in Africa or South America, Moses Hess and the leaders in Cologne saw that Jerusalem and Israel were the places where the Jewish state needed to be reborn. In many ways you could say that Moses Hess was preparing the way, one generation before Theodore Herzl, for the conception and rebirth of the State of Israel.

1896 – Theodore Herzl, the founder of modern-day Zionism, met William Heckler, a Christian Zionist and chaplain of the British Embassy in Vienna, Austria, in 1896. The providential meeting occurred while Herzl was working as a newspaper reporter on the Dreyfus case. Heckler initially and continually, for more than fifty years, encouraged Herzl and other Zionist leaders that their movement was of G-d.

Herzl and Heckler met one month after Herzl completed the book, *The Jewish State.* Heckler deduced that 1897 would mark the dawn of the final restoration of Israel in the promised land. Heckler announced this to princes, a statesman, and ecclesiastical dignitaries, and introduced many of them to Herzl. Herzl started publishing *Die Welt,* a weekly newspaper for the Zionist Movement, in 1896.

In August 1897, two hundred delegates met in Basel to hold the First Zionist Congress, and they founded the World Zionist Organization. Herzl predicted that within five to fifty years a Zionist State would be reestablished, which happened exactly fifty years later. Chaim Weizman, who later became the first president of Israel, lived and worked closely with Lord Balfour, a Christian Zionist in the British Government in London, to bring about the Balfour Declaration in 1917, paving the way for the rebirth of the nation of Israel thirty years later (see Appendix B).

1938 – Rees Howells, a Christian Zionist and great intercessor who headed a Bible school in Wales, had his students praying for the Jews for a long time, but in September 1938 he received a special burden from the Lord. When he heard that all the Jews had to leave Italy within six months and that anti-Semitism was rising rapidly in Germany, he turned his thoughts toward the return of the Jews to their homeland. He and his students prayed for hours and sometimes days at a time for the rebirth of Israel as a Jewish homeland. May G-d raise up others in our day to birth an even greater *Aliyah* movement and outpouring of the Spirit than happened in the first half of the previous century.

In 1985, ninety-seven years after Herzl, the first Christian Zionist Congress was held in Basel, Switzerland, and was attended by five hundred participants from all over the world. In 1988 on the fortieth anniversary of Israel's rebirth, the second Christian Zionist Congress was held in Jerusalem. The work of Christian Zionists has been a great encouragement to Zionism world wide, and as the nations become increasingly hostile toward Israel, the Christians are saying, "Israel, you are not alone."

Jewish and Christian Zionists alike are commanded in Psalm 122:6 to pray for the peace of Jerusalem, that G-d's *shalom* may be upon Jerusalem. Praying for the peace of Jerusalem is a responsibility for all of G-d's people throughout the world, and is the key to world redemption, reconciliation and restoration. May we be faithful to Him in obeying this commandment.

Isaiah 62:6-7 says, "I have posted watchmen on your walls, O Jerusalem; they will never be silent day or night." You who call on the Lord, give yourselves no rest and give Him no rest until He does two things: (1) Establishes Jerusalem—this happened in 1967 but is continuing through *Aliyah* from the nations and is the natural restoration of Zion; and, (2) makes Jerusalem the praise of all the earth, which is the spiritual restoration of Zion.

It is time for all Jews, but especially *Torah*-based Jewish people who are filled with the *Ruach HaKodesh* (Holy Spirit) of G-d, who know how to praise Him, to return to the Land and for the veil over the City of Jerusalem to be lifted and G-d's Glory to fall on Jerusalem. It is time for the ark of G-d's Presence to return to Jerusalem in unprecedented ways. This will happen as His redeemed people move into biblical praise and worship and break through the veil. Then His anointing will fall and break every yoke and the strongholds over Jerusalem and the glory of the Lord will cover the earth as the waters cover the seas.

In the 1990s and the first decade of the twentieth century we see the rise of Jewish leaders such as Rabbi Yehiel Eckstein, Rabbi Fass, and Rabbi David Rosen in Israel working strongly with Christians such as Debbie Kellogg in the USA to help with *Aliyah* and the support of Israel. Gentiles such as Ulf Ekman of Sweden and the late Gustav Scheller of England have also done notable work with the Jewish community in the former Soviet Union to promote *Aliyah*. Praise G-d. As Jewish and Christian Zionists, may we work together and find our destiny in G-d by following the example of those who went before us. May we be faithful in praying, warning, helping and participating in what may well be the last and hopefully the greatest wave of *Aliyah* in this century before severe judgements fall on America and other Gentile nations.

Isaiah 2:3 says the law will go forth from Zion and the word of the Lord from Jerusalem in the last days. May G-d give us the courage as Jewish and Christian Zionists to blow the trumpet in unison from Zion and sound the alarm together in America. Jewish people, come home to Jerusalem to worship and praise the High G-d of heaven with all your heart so He can make Jerusalem a "praise" in all the earth!

9

"Deliver Thyself, O Zion"–
Escape from the Daughter of Babylon

Deliver thyself, O Zion, that dwellest with from the daughter of Babylon (Zechariah 2:7 KJV).

Set up road signs; put up guideposts. Take note of the highway, the road that you take. Return, O Virgin Israel, return to your towns. How long will you wander, O unfaithful daughter? (Jeremiah 31:21)

"However, the days are coming," declares the LORD, "when men will no longer say, 'As surely as the LORD lives, who brought the Israelites up out of Egypt,' but they will say, 'As surely as the LORD lives, who brought the Israelites up out of the *land of the north* and out of all the countries [including America!] where he had banished them.' For I will restore them to the land I gave their forefathers. But now I will send for many fishermen," declares the LORD, "and they will catch them. After that I will send for many hunters, and they will hunt them down on every mountain and hill and from the crevices of the rocks" (Jeremiah 16:14-16).

And everyone who calls on the name of the LORD will be saved; for on Mount Zion and in Jerusalem there will be deliverance, as the LORD has said, among the survivors whom the LORD calls (Joel 2:32).

Every one of the eighty-eight civilizations of man's history has eventually fallen, many through corruption from within and others by an attack from without. The United States of America is one of the first major civilizations to last more than two hundred years (1776-2004) as a leading world power.

America has served as a great blessing to the Jewish people, and in many ways to the nations. However, its internal decay is beginning to eat away her strength. The decay of America has been increasing gradually over the last generation. As sin and decadence continue to accelerate, it is only by G-d's mercy that we have lasted this long as a world power.

Lester Sumrall said in his book, *Jerusalem: Where Empires Die* (1984):

> What has become of the United States since 1956? Note carefully. We have lost the last two wars we have fought, in Korea and Vietnam. Our society has begun to fall apart rapidly. Violent rebellion broke out on our college campuses. The drug problem, sexual sin, and divorce have exploded. Our economy has become far less stable and far more vulnerable to foreign competition.

> All these things may seem unrelated on the surface, but that is not the case. It is not a coincidence that these problems erupted after our desertion of Israel in 1956. And this turning away, however gradual, has continued in recent years as we have sought to please oil sheiks. Thus, like Babylon, Persia, Rome, and all the others, America has put its hand into the golden bowl of Jerusalem and is in imminent danger of being put on the shelf by G-d, so to speak, as a world power.

The beginning of 2004 is more than a generation (forty years) since the USA began turning its back on Israel. Will the US repeat the mistakes of England and stop supporting Israel after blessing her for hundreds of years? May G-d give America the grace to continue supporting Israel as she becomes the head and not the tail and a banner for the nations.

Sumrall continues:

> If there is no revival and renewed commitment to Israel, I can see the moral degradation of our day growing ever more

widespread and severe, and the United States decaying from within, as did Rome and many other great empires of the past. Perhaps then Russia and others could force us to our knees.

Also since 1956, prayer and Bible reading were removed from our schools and abortion was legalized in America. Unfortunately, not only is the secular American and international society today turning against Israel, but so is much of the nominal church. It was not until 1982 that G-d lifted the veil from my eyes to see His purposes for Israel in these last days. Because of my blindness in the past, I can empathize with many Christians who adhere to replacement theology today. We need to love them, pray for G-d to lift the veil from their eyes, and help them see the truth regarding G-d's purposes for Israel and the Jewish people today.

The story of the Church has been that many times the leaders of the last move of G-d rejected and persecuted the people who were in the forefront of G-d's ongoing purposes. The Catholics persecuted Luther; Luther and Calvin persecuted and condemned the killings of the Anabaptists; many of the traditional churches rejected the Jesus movement; the Assemblies of G-d initially rejected the Charismatic movement. Unless the veil is removed from Christians who believe in replacement theology, they could reject the coming outpouring of the Holy Spirit on Israel and even persecute the Jewish people.

If Catholic and Lutheran theology in many ways paved the way for the Inquisition and the Holocaust, I hate to think what kind of persecution could come in the near future toward the Jewish people unless G-d lifts the veil from the eyes of the nominal Christians. Nominal Christians and even born-again Christians, if blinded by replacement theology, could be fighting against Jerusalem and Jewish people even as they killed them in fighting for Hitler in Germany!

This is the word of the LORD concerning Israel. The LORD, who stretches out the heavens, who lays the foundation of the earth, and who forms the spirit of man within him, declares: "I am going to make Jerusalem a cup that sends all the surrounding peoples reeling. Judah will be besieged as well as Jerusalem. On that day, when

all the nations of the earth are gathered against her, I will make Jerusalem an immovable rock for all the nations. All who try to move it will injure [rupture] themselves. On that day I will strike every horse with panic and its rider with madness," declares the LORD. "I will keep a watchful eye over the house of Judah, but I will blind all the horses of the nations" (Zechariah 12:1-4).

This is the plague with which the LORD will strike all the nations that fought against Jerusalem: Their flesh will rot while they are still standing on their feet, their eyes will rot in their sockets, and their tongues will rot in their mouths (Zechariah 14:12).

Israel will be the next and last important civilization of man, according to the Bible. The land of Israel was given to the Jews as an everlasting and eternal possession as promised in Genesis 17:8. The Jewish patriarchs realized this, to the point they even had their bones buried there if they died outside Israel. It is again time to favor Zion. It is time to take the spiritual Ark back to Jerusalem. G-d will soon pour out greater judgements on America and other Gentile nations and a greater spiritual awakening will come on Israel.

People ask: Why did G-d allow the Holocaust in Europe? For years, a loving G-d warned the Jews to leave through the Jewish Zionist prophets, but ninety percent of them refused to leave before it was too late! If more than ten percent of the Jews leave America before it falls or becomes a lesser power, it would be one of the first times in history. Zechariah 12:8 says that two-thirds of the Jews in the world would be killed. One-third of them, six million, have already been killed in the Holocaust. I am concerned that six million more could be devastated in America unless they return soon.

G-d says in Jeremiah 16:16 that He will send for many fishers to warn and help them return to Israel. In Europe, the fishers were the Zionists and the hunters were the Nazis. Today in America, the fishers are the Jewish prophets as well as Christian Zionists. May the Jewish people respond to the fishers today or the hunters may soon come. In America they could be the KKK, Islamic terrorists or others.

This book is written with a deep love to warn the Jewish people to escape the Daughter of Babylon (the USA) because it is about to be greatly devastated. Precious Jewish people, if you don't leave immediately, you may go back with no money, you may be killed or not be able to go back at all!

Repeating what Santayana said: "He who does not learn from the lessons of history is doomed to repeat them." May the Jewish people and America as a nation learn from the recent lessons of history, may the Jewish people return to Israel very soon, and escape impending judgements and possible destruction in America.

Benefits of Making *Aliyah* Soon!

1. Honor the G-d of Israel and receive His blessing by obeying His call to return to the land of Israel.

2. Prepare for your children and succeeding generations to live in the land of promise. Many believe Israel will be the next and last important civilization of man before Messiah comes.

3. Escape the coming judgements and difficulties in the falling civilization of the USA.

4. If you return to Israel soon, you can take any finances with you before our economy falls. You can benefit and be a blessing by helping your family, but also the nation, by taking the wealth of the nations back to Israel. Prepare now to prosper in the land of your forefathers!

5. You can help restore the land to blossom as a rose in preparation for the return of millions of Jews from Russia and America in the coming years and welcome them home at the gates of Jerusalem.

6. Experience the blessings of living in the cultural and religious environment of your people and not being assimilated into Gentile cultures.

7. You can participate in the great Jewish Revival coming in the land of Israel as mentioned in Ezekiel 37 and welcome the Messiah.

Things to Do Immediately in Preparation for Making *Aliyah* Soon!

Every Jewish person in the United States (and the rest of the free world) should wisely and carefully do the following:

1. *Understand the Law of Return*: The State of Israel has a Law of Return, which allows all Jews to "return" to Israel and become citizens. (American Jews do not forfeit their US citizenship when they do this.) Also you can stay for an extended period of time on a visitor's passport or a work visa. Make your plans carefully and consult with knowledgeable people from your Congregation or organizations in Appendix D about *Aliyah*.

2. *Change your mind-set*: Remember that G-d Almighty has planned and declared that Jews are to be re-gathered and never again leave Israel:

> **"I will bring back my exiled people Israel; they will rebuild the ruined cities and live in them. They will plant vineyards and drink their wine; they will make gardens and eat their fruit. I will plant Israel in their own land, never again to be uprooted from the land I have given them," says the LORD your G-d (Amos 9:14-15).**

Living in the land of Israel is equal to all the other commandments in the *Torah* (Sifrey Re'eh 12:29 Mishnah).

3. *Get out of debt:* Pay off all accounts you owe, including credit cards.

4. *Get a passport:* Information can be obtained at your local post office about how to obtain a passport.

5. *Visit Israel.* See what the employment and housing situation is for each profession or vocation. Send for brochures if travel is beyond your budget. Seek out a few "pen pals" to answer your questions. You can also apply for *Aliyah* in Israel.

6. *Hebrew*: Start learning Hebrew while you are still in the *Galut* (Diaspora). Every bit helps. If possible, take a course that gives you an overview of the linguistic structure and grammar, because Israel's *ulpanim* (Hebrew-language training programs) do not do that. Since

most Americans, deep in their hearts, believe that English is the only "real" language in the world, learning Hebrew is their greatest single barrier to getting adjusted in Israel, so make it a priority.

7. *Marriage and children*: If you are single or married, childless or with a family, now is the time to immigrate. Every situation has its advantages so don't wait for a change—go as you are!

8. *Work*: Come with a profession if you can. Before investing years in training, check to see if your skills will be needed, how well such work pays, whether you will be able to work without broad knowledge of Hebrew, and whether it might be better to gain your particular job skills in Israel rather than in the *Galut*.

9. *Pull up your roots:* Solidify the value of your property in America and sell or at least buy an apartment or house in Israel. Only ship things that are necessary. You are better off buying many things once in Israel.

10. *Housing*: Save as much money as possible to buy property in Israel and buy as soon as possible! See Appendix D to plan for your and your family's future.

11. *Money*: Bring as much of your money and wealth of the nations back to bless Israel as possible, as Isaiah 60 says. You should invest as much money in Israel as possible while it can still be taken out of America.

12. *Pray:* Specifically pray for wisdom for the right place and exact time to make *Aliyah*. Pray also for the peace of Jerusalem (Psalm 122:6), and specifically for reconciliation and peace with G-d between Jews and Arabs.

Israel Come Home!

Afterwards the Israelites will return and seek the LORD their G-d and David their King. They will come trembling to the LORD and to His blessing in the last days (Hosea 3:5).

Be a pioneer and follow the Cloud of Glory like your Patriarchs:

Abraham, Moses, Joshua, David and others. Fulfill your end-time destiny as a son or daughter of Abraham and live as a practical Zionist in Israel, the land of your forefathers.

The Jews prospered greatly in historic Babylon as they have in America. G-d gave them a promise that Jeremiah spoke to the Jewish people in Babylon after the seventy years of captivity, if they were obedient to follow the Lord back to the land of Israel.

> **"For I know the plans I have for you," declares the LORD, "plans to prosper you and not to harm you, plans to give you hope and a future" (Jeremiah 29:11).**

I believe this is also applicable to the Jewish people who escape the Babylon of America today by returning to Israel. In Ezekiel 37:13-14, G-d says He will bring the Jewish people back to the land of Israel:

> **"Then you, my people, will know that I am the LORD, when I open your graves and bring you up from them. I will put my Spirit in you and you will live, and I will settle you in your own land. Then you will know that I the LORD have spoken, and I have done it," declares the LORD.**

Even though leaving America will mean some initial sacrifices and cultural changes, the question is not *if* you will have to make adjustments, but rather the question is whether you want to make the adjustments *now or later*—now at an easier time or at a more difficult time later. G-d promises a great spiritual revival in the land of Israel in the last days that will be much more meaningful and fulfilling than experiencing the economic, moral, military and spiritual disintegration—and possibly the soon destruction—of America! Beloved Jewish people, the apple of G-d's eye, don't miss your destiny in Zion! G-d of materialism, "LET MY PEOPLE GO!"

This third Exodus from the nations and return to Israel will be the greatest. It will bring forth what the first two only began preparing the way for. The third return will usher in the coming of Messiah in all His Glory, everlasting peace to Jerusalem, world redemption and the healing of the nations. It is no wonder Isaiah 51:11 (KJV) says:

> **Therefore, the redeemed of the LORD shall return, and**

come with singing unto Zion; and everlasting joy shall be upon their head: they shall obtain gladness and joy, and sorrow and mourning shall flee away.

G-d says in Zechariah 2:7:

"Come, O Zion! Escape, you who live in the Daughter of Babylon."

Precious Jewish people, make *Aliyah* very soon, don't wait until you *have to* go. Win the struggle and escape to Israel today. Come singing and dancing with joy and gladness to Zion preparing the way for the soon coming of your Messiah and King!

10

Update 1993

People, Get Ready, There's a Train or a Plane A-Coming!

In October of 1986, thirty-eight of us did a Jericho March around the Kremlin, believing G-d to break the strongholds binding the Jewish people in the USSR. In that year only about 200 Jews had been released from the USSR. A few days after our Jericho March in 1986, the Kremlin agreed to release 12,000 Jews. Every year for seven years the Lord has had us take another Jericho walk around the Kremlin. In 1988, 16,000 were released. The number rose to 70,000 in 1989 and over 200,000 were released in 1990, 1991, 1992 and 1993 from all the C.I.S. nations. The exodus about which Jeremiah prophesied three thousand years ago (Jeremiah 16:14-16) is happening.

During our 1987 trip, a group of watchmen did a Jericho March around the Atheist Museum in Leningrad, trusting G-d to break the walls of Communism. In 1990, the Communists tore the name "Atheism" off the museum, and they have now closed it completely and given it back to the church. (It was a cathedral before the 1907 Bolshevik Revolution.)

In 1988, on the fortieth year from the rebirth of Israel, we did our third Jericho March around the Kremlin in Moscow and gave out many clothes and around a thousand copies of this book in Russian.

During Passover of 1989, twenty-eight of us went to Russia to pray and work as "fishers" to bring the Jewish people home. G-d had spoken to me to help mobilize "fishers" to go to Russia. He'd burned on my heart the words of Jeremiah 16:16 (KJV): "Behold, I will send for many fishers." This Scripture did not apply to the exodus from Egypt or the partial return from Babylon, but it is referring to the situation today. G-d told me that a few fishers had gone forth, but now He is calling for many to go to Russia and all the nations where there are Jewish people, to warn them and help bring them home. Thousands of fishers were waiting for the "fish" (Jewish people) to come to Finland, but G-d said, "Go tell them to go across your border to Russia and bring them to Israel."

In 1990 we led our fifth mission to Moscow. Eighty of us, including twenty-eight from the International Christian Embassy in Jerusalem, went to Moscow, Leningrad, Odessa and Kiev to pray and conduct a concert tour calling and singing the Jewish people home to Israel.

Also on our 1990 trip, I led fifty-two intercessors to Odessa, where we prayed on the shores of the Black Sea for G-d to bring ships to Odessa to bring the Jews throughout Russia back to Israel. G-d answered our prayers through a Christian organization Ebenezer Emergency Fund, founded by Gustav Scheller (now deceased), which has to date brought one hundred thousand Jews back on ships from Odessa! Operation Jabotinsky, directed by Ulf Ekman also had a ship for this purpose.

In 1991 we took our sixth trip to Russia in the past six years and did our sixth Jericho March around the Kremlin, believing G-d for the walls of Communism to fall. We also prayed for the release of the Jewish people and for blessings to go into Russia. In December of 1991, the Soviet Union was dissolved and Mikhail Gorbachev resigned. G-d has answered our prayers, and the walls of Communism have collapsed.

In 1992 we had our seventh Jericho March around the Kremlin, with seven trumpet players to lead the way in celebration of the walls coming down. We prayed and believed G-d, as fishers, for the full release of the Jewish people and their homecoming (Jeremiah 16:16). Although more than five hundred thousand Jews have come home in the last few years, there are still millions who are still in Russia, the Ukraine and other countries that were part of the USSR.

We have taken more than thirty thousand Russian-language copies of *LET MY PEOPLE GO!* into Russia to encourage the Jews to come home. We are also believing G-d for the fullness of the Jewish people to return from the Ukraine by way of Odessa, on ships and also by planes! We also did a prayer mission in the former Yugoslavia two months before all the problems broke out, warning the Jewish people to flee Bosnia, Zagreb, Belgrade, Sarajevo—but they said they wanted to rebuild their culture. Only a few months later, they found themselves fleeing for their lives.

In the last couple of years, more copies of *LET MY PEOPLE GO!* have gone out in Russian than in English. Russian Jewish leaders are now requesting fifty thousand copies to be distributed in the USSR (a third printing). Fifty thousand additional copies were printed in 1994 in the Ukraine and are being distributed throughout the former USSR nations. According to these Jewish leaders, many are opting to come to Israel as a result of reading this book.

One of these leaders recently told me that the Fascism now emerging in the USSR resembles the atmosphere at the turn of the century when pogroms (massacres) broke out in seventy-five Russian cities and two million Jewish people fled to America. He believes if Russian nationalism continues to rise, it could be similar to that of the Nazi rule in Germany and Poland. Russian nationalism (*pamyat*) is the major anti-Semitic movement in Russia.

While anti-Semitism is in the Former Soviet Union, it has been growing in the United States over the past six years. We need to realize that the hunters (anti-Semites) are not only arising in Russia, but also in the West. The time of the fishers (Zionists, those helping and encouraging the Jews to return) is now, and the time of the hunters is at hand. The Jewish people have precious little time to escape from Russia and other nations before G-d allows more severe circumstances to push them homeward. The fishers must pray, warn and help so as many as possible can come home in this time of G-d's grace, before His fuller judgements are released on the Gentile nations!

LET MY PEOPLE GO!, released from the first printing in December 1987, is calling His people home, not only from Russia, but from the West as well. In America there could be an increase in economic problems that could unleash an anti-Semitism that people thought was impossible. The Jewish people must return to Israel soon in order to avoid being forced to return as refugees or being caught in the potential nuclear holocaust coming to the Gentile nation of America.

Dimitri Dudiman (now deceased), a prophet from the underground Church in Romania, had a vision of New York, Los Angeles and Miami being destroyed by nuclear missiles. If this happens, four million Jewish people could get caught in a nuclear holocaust meant for a Gentile nation— all because they didn't follow the seven hundred verses in the *Tanach* calling them home to Israel.

The hour is later than we think. In 1987, as I was driving into New York City, I saw in the Spirit many "cities of refuge" as Jewish people were fleeing the city. These cities of refuge are now being prepared. G-d directed me to Isaiah 60:22, which says that He will do this very swiftly. The swiftness of the changes in Eastern Europe and in the Former Soviet Union is a foreshadowing of the swiftness of the changes that could come in the West.

One day when I was praying, I saw a vision of a train leaving the station. The locomotive was the Lord leading the exodus from the "land of the north" (Jeremiah 16:15). The attached cars represented the Jewish people from all the other cities and nations, immediately following the locomotive. It is time for the Jewish people to get on the train coming out of Russia and the Ukraine, but also for them to get on the cars from New York, Los Angeles, Miami, Chicago, Boston, Baltimore, Philadelphia, Washington, D.C., San Francisco, Cleveland, Paris, Buenos Aires, London, Capetown, Toronto, Montreal, Budapest, Sydney, etc. Trains, cars and planes are bringing His people home to Israel! Israel will have her problems in the days ahead, but consider the following Scripture:

> **"And fear not, O Jacob My servant," declares the LORD, "and do not be dismayed, O Israel; for behold, I will save you from afar, and your offspring from the land of their captivity. And Jacob shall return, and shall be quiet and at ease, and no one shall make him afraid. For I am with you," declares the LORD, "to save you; for I will destroy completely all the nations where I have scattered you, only I will not destroy you completely. But I will chasten you justly, and will by no means leave you unpunished" (Jeremiah 30:10-11 NAS).**

As I was talking to a Russian Jew in Moscow, G-d gave me this simile: America is like a rose fully blossomed and turning dark, but Israel is like a rose just beginning to bud and blossom. Just prior to the writing of the 1993 edition, all the Jews were released from Albania in a few days and ninety-five percent of the Jews from Ethiopia within thirty-six hours.

I talked to an Orthodox Rabbi from New York on my last plane trip to the USA. I asked him if he planned to make *Aliyah* in the future, and he said that the Orthodox are planning a massive Aliyah from New York in the next few years. Many Jewish people who believe the Bible are now turning their eyes toward Jerusalem and planning their *Aliyah*. G-d is now bringing them home from the north, south, east and west.

In 1987, preceding Israel's fortieth birthday, our House of Prayer was born in Jerusalem. Watchmen have come to our "Jerusalem House of Prayer for all Nations" from over two hundred nations, basing their prayers on Isaiah 56:6-8:

> **"And foreigners who bind themselves to the LORD, to serve him, to love the name of the LORD and to worship him, all who keep the Sabbath without desecrating it and who hold fast to my covenant--these I will bring to my holy mountain and give them joy in my house of prayer. Their burnt offerings and sacrifices will be accepted on my altar; for my house will be called a house of prayer for all nations." The Sovereign LORD declares--he who gathers the exiles of Israel: "I will gather still others to them, besides those already gathered."**

We encourage watchmen and those who want to pray about *Aliyah* to join us in Jerusalem. Over the past few years, congregations in Israel and abroad have kept a continual fast, twenty-four hours a day, believing G-d to break the strongholds and bring His people home. G-d has heard our prayers and is answering.

The future of the Jewish people is in Israel. G-d's truth is marching onward toward Zion. All roads lead to Jerusalem! As the song says, "People get ready, there's a train a-coming!" It's picking up passengers from coast to coast and continent to continent. This last return will bring Messiah, blessing and peace to Jerusalem. Don't miss the train! Don't miss the plane! Get on board!

11

Update 1996

The *Shofar* is Sounding!

A t the time of the fifth writing of *LET MY PEOPLE GO!*, it was over ten years prior that we did our first of seven Jericho Marches around the Kremlin in 1986. That event happened just before G-d gave me the vision that led to writing the first edition of *LET MY PEOPLE GO!*. In 1986, only two hundred Jews had come home to Israel from the north (Russia and the former USSR). Over one million have come home during the ten years since then. This *Aliyah* will continue in increasing ways.

Since 1993, when chapter 11 was written, we have led prayer teams, conducted Jericho Marches, and encouraged the Jewish people to come home from all the parts of the world to which they have been scattered. We also are holding a "Breakthrough Fast" over Passover each year in Jerusalem. This is sponsored by the Jerusalem House of Prayer for All Nations, and is joined by groups in over one hundred nations.

Redemptive Judgements in the USA

Although we have seen many Jews come home from the South (nations such as Ethiopia, South Africa and Yemen) and from the East (nations such as India and China), the question remains: What about the West? Eighty percent of all Jews outside Israel today live in the West. G-d is about to begin to shake the West in a much fuller way, beginning with the USA, where even more Jewish people live than in Israel.

In October 1996, after sponsoring the "All Nations Convocation Jerusalem" which was attended by pastors and prayer leaders from a hundred and eighty-eight nations, I flew to Charlotte, North Carolina, to speak at a Morning Star conference with Rick Joyner. It turned out that a major emphasis of the conference was on Israel! I was shocked to hear that Jim Bakker, who had been recently released from prison, would be speaking at this conference held on the former ground of his Heritage USA complex. But Jim's message was truly one of the most prophetic messages I have ever heard. He shared how G-d had radically dealt with him in prison as he read the Bible eight to sixteen hours a day. He called us to be converted to the real Gospel and to the real Messiah.

When I went for a walk the next morning, I began to weep and G-d began to speak to me. He reminded me that it had only been a few hours before the exposure on March 19, 1987, of the incident involving Jim Bakker and Jessica Hahn, that He had spoken to me about the judgement at the door for the American Church (mentioned in Chapter 1 of this book). Five days later, on March 24, 1987, I had the vision referred to in the first chapter of this book, depicting severe judgement about to fall on the USA and an urgency that the Jewish people be warned to return to Israel. I continued weeping as I walked the grounds of the former Heritage USA and pondered how the Lord had spoken to me nearly ten years earlier. I saw that in 1987 judgement began to fall on the church.

Judgement is at the door! I sense that Jim Bakker's experiences and G-d's dealing with him were the "first fruits" of what the church will have to go through due to the shakings in America in the coming years. Yet G-d has purposed not only to purify the church in the USA, but also to bring the Jewish people home to Israel.

G-d recently put in my hands Dietrich Bonhoeffer's books written in prison, *Life Together* and *The Jesus Family in Communist China*. They are a powerful message for our times. G-d wants the true believers prepared for the trials that lie ahead and ready for His coming. He wants the tens of millions in the USA who have had counterfeit conversions to be converted to the real Gospel, so that the fullness of the authentic harvest can come in and be reaped!

It is G-d's mercy to shake America to fulfill His purposes. One of the major results of the coming shakings (judgements) and the collapse of the G-d of mammon in the USA is that the Jewish people will be released. Anti-Semitism will grow as Jews will become scapegoats. I believe economic shakings, increased terrorism, earthquakes, and possibly war are coming soon.

Just after the Charlotte conference in October 1996, I went shopping to buy some clothes. When I saw a sweater that had "USA" on the front in big red letters, I began weeping as I saw judgements coming on her. I was impressed to buy the sweater to remind me to pray for the deliverance of the Jewish people from America to Israel and to their Messiah. I was reminded that having a burden for Israel means also having a burden for the USA, since more Jews are in the USA than in Israel.

As I was leaving Charlotte for Moravian Falls, North Carolina, where I believe angels are waiting to assist the Archangel Michael in bringing the Jews home from the USA, I turned on the radio and the first song I heard was the Byrds' classic, "Turn, Turn, Turn." Based on Ecclesiastes 3, the song says there is a season for everything under heaven—a time for peace and a time for war. I started weeping again. Seconds later, I turned my head to the left and saw a large sign which said "Jeremiah's," and I wept even more.

As I reached the mountains of Moravian Falls, G-d spoke to me that the time is coming for Isaiah 60 and 61 to be fulfilled. Isaiah 60:22 says:

"The least of you will become a thousand, the smallest a mighty nation. I am the LORD; in its time I will do this *swiftly.***"**

This is in the context of the Jewish people coming home, and the first verse of Isaiah 61 speaks about the Year of Jubilee. Deep darkness is coming, but also great glory. The Lord will bring His people home from the West. The Lion of Judah, is about to roar in Israel!

"They will follow the LORD; *he will roar like a lion.* **When he roars, his children will come trembling** *from the west.* **They will come trembling like birds from Egypt, like doves from Assyria. I will settle them in their homes," declares the LORD (Hosea 11:10-11).**

Dark Clouds

As we began the Year of Jubilee, fifty years since the rebirth of the nation of Israel, He began to bring shakings that will bring His people home! He also showed me Isaiah 5:26-30:

> **He lifts up a banner for the distant nations, he whistles for those at the ends of the earth. Here they come, *swiftly and speedily*! Not one of them grows tired or stumbles, not one slumbers or sleeps; not a belt is loosened at the waist, not a sandal thong is broken. Their arrows are sharp, all their bows are strung; their horses' hoofs seem like flint, their chariot wheels like a whirlwind. Their roar is like that of the lion, they roar like young lions; they growl as they seize their prey and carry it off with no one to rescue. In that day they will roar over it like the roaring of the sea. And if one looks at the land he will see darkness and distress; even the light will be *darkened by the clouds*.**

He said that we would be whistling them home and I believe that warfare worship will help to prepare the way for their release. At Moravian Falls I found myself whistling the songs, "Year of Jubilee," "Battle Hymn of the Republic," and "Blow the Trumpet in Zion." As I was doing this, two eagles flew overhead. After the first eagle flew past, a *Shofar* sounded and then another *Shofar* sounded after the second eagle passed! These were as if blown by angels and were heard by those with me!

A Time for Action

If you are Jewish, it is time to come home as soon as possible. If you are a Christian, it is time for the Church in the West to watch and pray. Be purified, and prepare for the coming shakings. Warn the Jewish people and help them come home to Israel before and during the crisis that is coming!

Experiencing the fullness of your destiny is based on how you respond. Help and bless His chosen people to fulfill *their* destiny in following the seven hundred scriptures calling them home to their land and to their Messiah.

> **I will bless those who bless you [my people] and whoever curses you I will curse (Genesis 12:3).**

Jewish people, prepare to leave! Christians, get prepared to help them leave!

I am the LORD; it its time I will do this *swiftly* **(Isaiah 60:22).**

For the LORD will rebuild Zion and appear in his glory (Psalm 102:16).

We see the mention of *dark clouds* in Psalm 97:2, and this is symbolic of war:

Clouds and thick darkness **surround him; righteousness and justice are the foundation of his throne.**

See, *darkness* **covers the earth and** *thick darkness* **is over the peoples, but the LORD rises upon you and his glory appears over you (Isaiah 60:2).**

...to proclaim the year of the LORD's favor [Year of Jubilee] and the day of vengeance of our G-d, to comfort all who mourn (Isaiah 61:2).

In that day they will roar over it like the roaring of the sea. And if one looks at the land, he will see *darkness* **and distress; even the light will be darkened by the clouds (Isaiah 5:30).**

...a day of *darkness and gloom,* **a day of** *clouds and blackness* **(Joel 2:2).**

Washington's Word of Warning

George Washington's vision regarding the "Third Peril"[1] states:

"Again I heard the mysterious voice saying, 'Son of the Republic, look and learn.' At this the dark shadowing angel *put the trumpet [Shofar] to his mouth* and blew three distinct blasts. Taking water from the ocean he sprinkled it upon Europe, Asia and Africa. Then my eyes beheld a fearful scene. From each of these continents arose *thick black clouds* that were soon joined into one. And throughout this mass there gleamed a dark red light by which I saw hordes of armed men. These men moving with the cloud, marched by land, and sailed by sea to America which was enveloped in the volume of the cloud. And I dimly saw these vast armies devastate the whole country. And burned the villages, towns and cities which I had seen springing up. As my ears listened to the thundering of the cannon, flashing of swords and the shouts and cries of millions in mortal combat, I again heard the mysterious voice saying, 'Son of the Republic, look and learn.' When the voice had ceased, the *angel placed the trumpet [Shofar] once more to his mouth* and blew a long and fearful blast.

"Instantly a light as of a thousand suns shone down from above me, and pierced and broke into fragments the dark cloud which enveloped America. At the same moment the angel upon whose head still shone the word 'Union,' and who bore our national flag in one hand and a sword in the other, descended from the heavens attended by legions of white spirits. These immediately joined the inhabitants of America, who I perceived were well-nigh overcome, but who immediately taking courage again, closed up their broken ranks and renewed the battle. Again, amid the fearful noise of the conflict, I heard the mysterious voice saying, 'Son of the Republic, look and learn.' As the voice ceased, the shadowy angel for the last time dipped water from the ocean and sprinkled it upon America. Instantly the dark cloud rolled back, together with the armies it had brought, leaving the inhabitants of the land victorious."

Anthony Sherman climaxed his recollection of Washington's words by saying, "Such, my friends, were the words I heard from Washington's own lips, and America will do well to profit by them."

Thomas Jefferson once said of our first President: "His integrity was the most pure, his justice the most flexible, I have ever known. He was, indeed, in every sense of the word, a wise, a good and a great man."

Interpretation of the Vision

The "Third Peril" seen by Washington, the last and most terrible of all, clearly predicts hordes of enemies from Europe, Asia and Africa, armed for mortal combat. A red light accompanies these terrible invaders—

indicating they are no doubt Muslims or Communists. They come by air (the cloud), land (perhaps via Canada) and sea. They devastate *all* of America, destroying cities, towns and villages. Millions are engaged in mortal conflict.

The words from Joel 3:9 are for this time! Proclaim this among the nations. Prepare for war! Arouse the warriors! Let all the men draw near and attack. Beat your plowshares into swords and your pruning hooks into spears. Let the weakling say, "I am strong." Bring down your warriors, O Lord!

This scripture applies not only to the USA, but also to Israel. During the twenty-one days I was outside of Israel in the USA, I was in an almost constant state of being stunned. Many times, especially when I was alone, I would just begin to weep. I wept more over these twenty-one days than any time in my life!

The Lord showed me I had to fly back to Israel as soon as the elections were over—the night of November 5, 1996. This truly was the anointed time. I flew on TWA from New York, on the same route as the TWA plane which crashed a few months before.[1] Something very amazing happened. As we were boarding the plane, *someone sounded a Shofar!* I had never heard this in any airport anywhere and I've flown more than a thousand flights! Then we sat in the plane for almost one and a half hours because of problems with the plane at which point it was announced that Clinton won the election. *Then someone again sounded the Shofar* on the plane as it departed from New York to Israel.

I asked different people if they heard these two *Shofar* blasts and they did, but no one knew who it was. It was was as if an angel blew the shofars as in the mountains of North Carolina twelve days before, mentioned earlier in this writing, who blew two different times. This reminded me of the *Shofar* being blown at two different times by an angel is also in George Washington's vision! The Lord seems to have confirmed His word by angels blowing the *Shofar* on three different occasions: At George Washington's vision of "The Third Peril"(see Chapter 2), when I was in Moravian Falls, and when the plane was leaving New York for Israel.

It truly is the time for the American Jews to return to Israel. It is the Year of Jubilee and the vengeance of our G-d (Isaiah 61:2). The Lord is blowing the *Shofar* and warning of danger, judgement and possible war. He is calling His people home before the great shaking on the USA. There is little time left for the Jews to come home to Israel with G-d's blessing. If they remain in the USA much longer, they may get caught in the imminent judgements upon America, or they may have to come back as refugees, as have the ninety percent who have come home from the nations to Israel since 1948.

In April 1987, we prayed in Moscow for the Archangel Michael to arise and bring Jews home from the Soviet Union. Then the breakthrough there began and over one million have returned to Israel from the Former Soviet Union since that time.

April 1997 was also a very significant month. When I was in the Dominican Republic the Lord spoke to me, "505 – 50," that in 1492, 505 years earlier, when Columbus discovered and immigrated to America - to the Dominican Republic - that he and others with him had Jewish blood and that this was the beginning of the dispersion of the Jews to The Americas. I was also impressed that in this place where Columbus is buried, as a shofar was blown, G-d was saying "50" represents Jubilee, time to return, which He said was soon to begin in the natural for Israel and also for *Aliyah* from the West; the Lord setting the Jewish captives free to bring them home to Israel.

Later I saw the movie "Prince of Egypt" at 5:05 PM. Then at 5:50 pm I flew from New York to Moscow and at 5:50 am arrived back in Tel Aviv. I sensed an open heaven in Moscow. I believe a new wave of *Aliyah* and revival like that which has come from Russia will be joined with an *Aliyah* from the West - USA. We pray for Michael to arise in the USA and bring the Jews home from the USA to Israel at the appointed time (see Ezekiel 17:1-10).

After I returned to Israel the next morning at 3:00 a.m. the Lord woke me up and said, "Look at your license plate on your new car." As I opened the door, I was stunned to see it said "505-50-19." The Lord has been bringing 505 and 550 to me many times since then.

In November of 1997, we held All Americas Convocation in Miami, with delegates representing forty nations of The Americas. The Watchmen from the Dominican Republican came and blew the shofar for the return of the Jews from the Americas and we prayed for the Gates to open for the Jews from Miami and all the Americas to come home to Israel.

Seven years later in 2004, on the day we decided to print, we experienced the worst earthquake in Jerusalem in seventy-seven years. On that day we had received enough money to print, package, and mail 550,000 books to 550,000 Jewish households. This occurred during the fifty-fifth year since the birth of Israel and the year the author's fifty-fifth year of life.

The Lord wants to set the captives free from not only Russia (the North), but also the South, the East and especially New York, the USA and the West! Pray and work with us that the Lord will now begin to set Jews free from the Americas (the West) before it's too late.

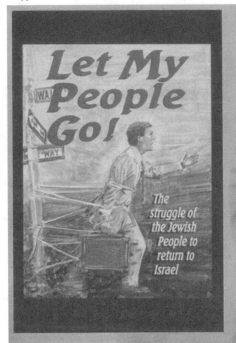

Let My People Go!

The struggle of the Jewish People to return to Israel

Walking away from Wall Street on Sept. 11th, 2001.
(Adapted from *L.A. Times* 2001)

Shake off your dust, free yourself from your cords, O captive daughter of Zion (Isaiah 52:2).

Update 2004

After September 11th, 2001 —Another Warning

In the year 2001, as we began a new millennium, Ariel Sharon became Prime Minister of Israel. His name, "Ariel" means "Lion of G-d." The G-d of Israel, the Lion of the tribe of Judah, has truly begun to roar into the new millennium. We have seen great shakings in New York City, the city with the largest Jewish population in the world, shakings in Jerusalem, and shakings throughout Israel. The World Trade Center collapsed, Islam is being shaken in Israel, and the Israeli government and Prime Minister Ariel Sharon says he is preparing for one million US Jews to make *Aliyah* to Israel.

On September 11th 2001, five days before Rosh Hashanah, the first Jewish New Year in the new millennium—the 21st Century—New York, USA, the daughter of Babylon (USA), was shaken in a way unparalleled in its two hundred and fifty year history. It will never be the same! Two airplanes were hijacked and used as weapons by Islamic terrorists. Each hit one of the Twin Towers of the World Trade Center in New York City, the "Big Apple," the biggest Jewish city in the world, and the most potent symbols of the greatness of New York City, the USA, and the world. The terrorist attack completely destroyed the buildings, thought to be indestructible, and killed over three thousand victims. Within the same hour, two other airplanes were also hijacked. One hit the Pentagon, destroying a section of the building and killing another one hundred and eighty-nine persons both on the ground and in the airplane. The fourth plane, thought to be heading for the White House or Three Mile Island in Pennsylvania, crashed before hitting its target.

This surely was a roar of the lion and a wake-up call and warning to the USA as a whole, to the Christian Church, and especially to both in relation to the Jewish people and the message of this book. It is a final warning of the imminent fall of Babylon as Revelation 18:10 says, **"In one hour Babylon will begin to fall."** This may be a final wake-up call for Jews in the USA and other nations to come home to Israel before further calamities come.

Israel is the final destiny and safest place on earth for the Jewish people. It is a myth that the Jews are safer in the USA or other nations than in Israel. To think this is a belief in a big lie. Jewish people, who were on a Solidarity Mission in Israel, would have been killed while working in the Twin Towers if they had not come to visit Israel. More people were killed in NYC in one hour by Muslim terrorists than all the terror attacks in Israel in the last seven years.

On September 11th the Liberal National Council of Churches in New York was to begin a three-day conference to propagate replacement theology and to rebuke the State of Israel for not giving away their land to the Muslims, but the meeting never began because of the terrorist strike! Truly G-d is rebuking the numbed Church and calling her to repentance.

In 2001, after living in Jerusalem for fifteen years, we hosted a convocation for two weeks with thirteen hundred delegates, beginning only five days after the September 11th Islamic attack on America. Although the conditions for travel were difficult, the delegates who came from the nations were like modern-day Joshuas and Calebs. They believed the report of the Lord that Israel is a "good land flowing with milk and honey" and that "we are more than able to possess it." The delegates at the convocation visited all the cities and regions of the land, and prayed for G-d's intervention and blessing. They returned to their nations praying for many to be freed from fear in their nations.

When I moved to Jerusalem in 1987 from Washington D.C., people said, "Are you crazy? Don't you know it is dangerous in Jerusalem, Israel?" I decided to do a statistical analysis and found, to my surprise, that over ten times as few people were killed that year and most years since in Jerusalem than in Washington D.C., a city of about the same size. I thought that my friends in Washington should maybe move to Israel with me if they were scared of dying!

---

1. End-Time Handmaidens, Inc. "Washington's Vision"

We can see that since 1939 over seven million Jews were killed by terrorism in the nations, including the Holocaust, and less than twenty thousand in all the wars and terrorism in Israel put together. The reality is that over the last sixty-two years it has been three hundred times safer for a Jew to live in Israel than in the nations. The percentage of Jews killed in the nations is 99.7% and while 45% of all the Jews in the world live in Israel only 0.3% of all Jews killed have been killed in Israel.

In the opinion of the author in relation to what G-d showed on March 24, 1987, in Chapter 1 of this book, September 11th, 2001, in the USA was far more than a wake-up call (Luke 21). I was told that "Severe judgements are coming on America soon, but I am holding them back briefly, because the Jews have not been adequately warned to come home to Israel." September 11th, 2001 was a sign that much greater shakings and judgements are coming, but G-d is holding them back very briefly, because the Jews must be adequately warned.

After September 11th, 2001, is the time for the Jews to be given a final warning and for the fishers to warn and help Jews to come home. G-d is now speaking: **Behold, now I send for many fishers [to the USA] (Jeremiah 16:16)** to help bring the Jews home to Israel.

September 11th was also a sign of a major paradigm shift in the heavenlies and on earth as the first Jewish New Year in the new millennium began only a few days after and G-d is saying the times of the Gentiles are soon coming to an end. Jeremiah 30:11 says, **"I am with you, and will save you, declares the LORD. Though I completely destroy all the nations among which I scatter you, I will not completely destroy you."** G-d declares that He will not completely destroy Israel.

Jacob's great trouble in the last days is set forth in Jeremiah 30 (read whole chapter) and surely it began with the Holocaust in Europe as six million Jews were killed by Hitler. In this same chapter of Jeremiah, G-d shows that He wants to save His people out of Jacob's trouble in a distant land (USA) and other nations in the last days. He wants to break the yokes and bonds of Babylonian captivity materialism and slavery off their necks and bring them home to Israel if they are willing. Psalm 110:3 promises that He will cause His people to be willing in the day of His power.

Zechariah 13:8-9 says that two-thirds of the Jews in the world will be killed and only one-third will come home, and survive through the fire in Israel. Six million Jews, one-third, were killed by Hitler, another six million Jewish babies by abortion, and another six million and many more could still be killed in the nations. Eighty percent of Jews in the world today living outside Israel live in the USA. This is by far the most distant and largest of all major Jewish communities outside Israel. I realize one of the reasons the USA is under attack is because even more Jews live there than in Israel. They are under the greatest threat and should come home very soon.

Jeremiah 30:11 says:

"I am with you and will save you," declares the LORD. "Though I completely destroy all the nations among which I scatter you, I will not completely destroy you."

In addition to the Jewish Agency and Israeli groups like AACI and Tehilla, a new organization, Nefesh B'Nefesh, began offering Jewish people from the USA $5,000 to $25,000 dispersed over the first three years after making *Aliyah* to Israel. Ezekiel 36:8 says, **"But you, O mountains of Israel, will produce branches and fruit for my people Israel, for they will soon come home."** In the summer of 2002 over one thousand North Americans made *Aliyah*. The largest group ever to make *Aliyah* from the USA in the history of Israel landed in 2002 through Nefesh B'Nefesh. They continued to arrive from the USA in increasing measure in 2003 while the numbers continued to decrease from the former Soviet Union marking a paradigm shift since the summer of 2002. The heartland of Israel—Judea and Samaria—and the West Bank will soon be filled with Jewish people where G-d made covenantal promises: Here are the natural pillars and foundations of the House of Israel, with Abraham, Isaac and Jacob.

Micah 5:3-5 says, **"Therefore Israel will be abandoned [alone] until the time when she who is in labor [Israel] gives birth and the rest of his brothers return to join the Israelites. He will stand and shepherd His flock in the strength of the LORD, in the majesty of the name of the LORD his G-d. And they will live securely for then his greatness will**

---

1. *Time Magazine*, August 5, 1996, "Crash Investigation: The Search for Sabotage" p.26

reach to the ends of the earth and he will be their peace." The time is coming soon when it seems even as the Bible says, the USA and all nations will abandon Israel.

> On that day I will make the leaders of Judah like a brazier [fire pot] in a woodpile, like a flaming torch among sheaves. They will consume right and left all the surrounding peoples, but Jerusalem will remain intact in her place.

> The Lord will save the dwellings of Judah first, so that the honor of the house of David and of Jerusalem's inhabitants may not be greater than that of Judah. On that day the LORD will shield those who live in Jerusalem, so that the feeblest among them will be like David and the house of David will be like G-d, like the Angel of the LORD going before them. On that day I will set out to destroy all the nations that attack Jerusalem (Zechariah 12:6-9).

> "For I know the plans I have for you," declares the LORD, "plans to prosper you and not to harm you, plans to give you hope and a future. Then you will call upon me and come and pray to me, and I will listen to you. You will seek me and find me when you seek me with all your heart. I will be found by you," declares the LORD, "and I will bring you back from captivity. I will gather you from all the nations and places where I have banished you," declares the LORD, "and will bring you back to the place from which I carried you into exile." (Jeremiah 29:11-14)

> You who have escaped the sword, leave and do not linger! Remember the LORD in a distant land, and think on Jerusalem (Jeremiah 51:50).

> Cargoes of cinnamon and spice, of incense, myrrh and frankincense, of wine and olive oil, of fine flour and wheat; cattle and sheep; horse and carriages; and bodies and souls of men.

> They will say, "The fruit you longed for is gone from you. All your riches and splendor have vanished, never to be recovered." The merchants who sold these things and gained their wealth from her, will stand far off, terrified at her torment. They will weep and mourn and cry out:

> 'Woe! Woe, O great city, dressed in fine linen, purple and scarlet, and glittering with gold, precious stones and pearls! In one hour such great wealth has been brought to ruin! (Revelation 18:13-17)

Ezekiel was written after the exodus from Egypt. From this scripture we can see the day is coming when every Jew in the world will be living in Israel. This means that the only place the Jews will be alive on earth will be Israel. Israel will be not only the safest place for the Jews to live, but also the only place they will live.

> Then they will know that I am the LORD their G-d, for though I sent them into exile among the nations, I will gather them to their own land, not leaving any behind. I will no longer hide my face from them, for I will pour out my Spirit on the house of Israel, declares the Sovereign LORD (Ezekiel 39:28-29).

In the 1940s, the S/S St. Louis, a ship carrying more than nine hundred Jewish passengers, was rejected by three counties in the State of Florida and sent back to Europe to die in the Holocaust. In November 2000 as I was in Israel watching the US presidential elections, I realized that the three counties that had rejected the S/S St. Louis were the very three counties where the elections were delayed due to controversy over the votes. G-d showed that He allowed this to get our attention because there is a need to repent for this root sin of rejecting the Jews of the S/S St. Louis and sending them back to the Holocaust.

In June 2001 we convened the All Americas Convocation for repentance from the Church and nations of the Americas. Sixty-two survivors, including spouses, from the S/S St. Louis who returned to Europe and escaped death in the Holocaust, attended the convocation. Leaders of the nations in the Americas asked forgiveness for rejecting them from the

USA. There was much weeping and repentance, and a sovereign joining of the Jewish and Christian communities that is needed to help prepare the way for *Aliyah* from the West. At that time we took an offering of about $100,000 towards mailing the book *LET MY PEOPLE GO!*

In March 2002 we brought twelve survivors of the S/S St. Louis to Israel, most for the first time, and repented at Yad V'Shem and at the Lighting of the Eternal Flame.

We believe that one redemptive purpose of G-d allowing the tragedy of September 11th to happen, was to begin to prepare the way for a final warning for the six million Jews in the USA to return to their homeland, Israel, and to prevent another Jewish tragedy like the Holocaust. *Aliyah* can be completed to prepare the way for the Lord, the King of Glory (Psalm 102:16).

Like the two shofars heard in George Washington's vision, I heard two shofars being blown as if by angels in 1996 when I was in travail in Moravian Falls, North Carolina, USA. Following that in the same week, when I flew to Israel from New York, which is when intelligence reports in Jerusalem said the plans to destroy the twin towers began, I again heard two shofars at the airport and on the plane. Hosea 11:10 says,

"They will follow the LORD; he will roar like a lion. When he roars, his children shall come trembling from the west."

At George W. Bush's inaugural speech in Washington D.C. in January 2001, the first month of the new millennium, he quoted Thomas Jefferson's words written at the time of the Declaration of Independence and the Revolutionary War: "We know the race is not to the swift nor to the strong. Do you not think an angel rides in the whirlwind and directs this storm." Bush continued, "An angel still rides in the whirlwind and directs this storm." Just after this, two shofars were heard being blown at Bush's presidential inauguration with no one in sight blowing them. Could it be that they were blown by angels as a sign of G-d's direction and help for the coming storm Bush would face eight months later and as another final warning for Jews in the USA to come home before it is too late?

An article from the *Five Jewish Towns Newspaper* in Long Island,

New York, showed how G-d sovereignly got some Jewish people out of the World Trade Center. They were praying on the ninety-ninth floor and the shofar blower realized that he had forgotten his shofar. After the prayer he asked them to follow him down to his office on the fiftieth floor. A few minutes after the shofar blasts were heard, the first plane hit the World Trade Center just above. These Jewish people escaped after blowing the shofar as another final call of deliverance for the Jewish people to come back to Israel and G-d.

In October 2001, I once again heard shofars sound as if by angels on Mount Zion and on the Mount of Olives in Jerusalem. Psalm 102:16 says:

"For the LORD will build up Zion and appear in His glory [to the Mount of Olives.]"

Aliyah is connected to the return of the Lord as Hosea 11:10-11 says:

"They will follow the LORD; he will roar like a lion. When he roars, his children shall come trembling from the west. They will come trembling like birds from Egypt, like doves from Assyria. I will settle them in their homes, declares the LORD."

In June 2001, G-d showed me that the time is imminent to fully release the message of *Aliyah* to the USA and the West. More watchmen (fishers) and Jewish people are hearing the shofars sounding and releasing a clearer call for Jews everywhere to come home to their land and G-d; to come home with their finances before it's too late.

Now Argentina is trembling and many are coming home due to great economic shaking and rising anti-Semitism. France is now trembling as bombs have been exploding in Paris, Lyon, Strasbourg and Marseilles. New York was trembling and will tremble as modern Israel is ending its fifty-sixth year. On March 24th 1987, as mentioned in the first chapter of this book G-d spoke to me "Severe judgements are coming on America soon, but I am holding them back briefly, because the Jews have not been adequately warned." This is a final warning.

In 2002, for the first time in history more Jews came to Israel from the West than from the Former Soviet Union or other parts of the world.

The *Aliyah* offices in New York said more Jews are applying for *Aliyah* than before. Something is happening. It is G-d's time for the Jews in the West and all nations to come home to Israel.

On December 26th, 2002, I had a revelation that I sent to President Bush and Prime Minister Ariel Sharon that I believe was a warning from G-d that if the US went against Iraq with a predetermined commitment *to divide up* G-d*'s chosen land*, Israel, by making an Islamic-Palestinian State, then they would have many problems in Iraq and judgement could come against the United States as the prophet Joel said in Joel 3:1-2.

In those days and at that time, when I restore the fortunes of Judah and Jerusalem, I will gather all nations and bring them down to the Valley of Jehoshaphat. There *I will enter into judgement against them concerning my inheritance, my people Israel, for they* scattered my people among the nations and *divided up my land*.

On February 1st, 2003, when the US space shuttle crashed over Palestine, Texas, only a few miles from Bush's Texas home, with an Israeli astronaut who bombed Iraq and US astronauts on board, I had another revelation. As terrible as the accident was, I believe that it was a second warning from G-d: If the USA and Israel try to create an Islamic-Palestine State, then similar to the Oslo Accords, this too could become a disaster for the USA and Israel, because it is against G-d's word in the Bible. It is even possible that President Bush could be removed from office for going against G-d's word. G-d has his peace plan for Israel and the Middle East that will not fail. G-d's peace plan is mentioned in Isaiah 19:23-25 and Psalm 87. To understand G-d's Abrahamic covenants with Israel, read the Holy Spirit birthed road map of reconciliation, G-d*'s Abrahamic Covenants with Israel* by Tom Hess.

On August 15th, 2003, the worst blackout in US history caused all the lights to go out for two days in New York City and much of the Northeast US where most of the Jews in the USA live. Many said that the darkness in New York gave a very erie feeling. It says in Revelation 18:23,

"The light of a lamp will never shine in you again. The voice of a bridegroom and bride will never be heard in

**you again. Your merchants were the world's great men.
By your magic spell all the nations were led astray."**

Could the black out be another final warning that it is time for the American Jews to come home? On night of my last revision of this text, February 14, 2004, President Bush said biological, nuclear and chemical weapons are still a threat to the USA.

It is time to invest in Israel. It is time to buy homes and real estate, invest in Israeli bonds. Prepare for the future and destiny of you and your family in your homeland Israel.

On September 29th, 2003, exactly three years to the day that fifteen hundred leaders were arriving in Israel on planes from two hundred nations and the day the second *Intifada* broke out, intercessors from the nations were gathered at the Ramat Rachel Hotel to pray. That night I spoke on *Aliyah* and along with Ulf Ekman received an offering of fifty-five thousand US dollars for *Aliyah*. The same night (his birthday), the former mayor of Jerusalem and current Vice-Prime Minister, Ehud Olmert, addressed the World Wide Watch Convocation 2003.

October 31st, 2003, in the Los Angeles area, the area of the second largest Jewish community in the world, a terrible fire broke out killing many people. The fire was the worst in history in this area and could be a sign to the Jews in Los Angeles as it was in Europe to Max Nordau who said, "The fire is burning under your feet" or when Jabotinsky said, "Liquidate the Diaspora or the Diaspora will liquidate you!"

Not only is the shofar sounding louder and clearer than ever, but the Lion is roaring louder than ever. When the Lion roars, His people will come trembling from the West (Hosea 11:10-11). This is a final warning to the Jews in New York and the rest of the USA.

Micah 2:13 says, in relation to *Aliyah*:

**One who breaks open the way will go up before them;
they will break through the gate and go out. Their king
will pass through before them, the LORD at their head.**

G-d is shaking everything that can be shaken. It is time for Jewish people to break free to Israel. The way has been prepared!

They will follow the Lord;
He will roar like a lion.

When the Lion roars His people will come
trembling from the West (Hosea 11:10,11)

13

Update 2009

After the Wall Street Crash of 2008 — Final Warning

Welcome Home to Israel

In Isaiah 43, G-d says He will bring the Jews home from the North, South, East and West. While most of the Jews have come home from the rest of the world, 85-90% of the Jews living outside Israel today, arc in the West, and primarily in the USA. I believe Jeremiah 30:10, when it speaks of G-d bringing the Jews from a distant place in the last days, is Aliyah from the USA, seeing as two-thirds of the Jews outside of Israel live there. Europe and Russia are only 3 or 4 hour flights from Israel, while the USA is 11-15 hours – truly a distant place.

The Twin Towers Fall

On September 11th, 2001, the Lion roared over the USA in regards to terrorism. I happened to be watching CNN when the Twin Towers fell and saw the great shaking this brought to the USA. This terrible event not only brought down the World Trade Center, but killed thousands of people in New York City, by far the city with the largest Jewish population in the world. This was another sign that the home of the Jewish people is not in the USA but in Israel. The Lion of Judah continues roaring with the purpose of bringing His people home to Israel and G-d.

Aliyah has continued to increase since that time. Soon after 9/11, the first full planeload of Jewish people from the US made Aliyah to Israel. Dozens more planeloads have come home to Israel since then. In 2008, for the first time in over 2000 years, Israel once again secured the largest Jewish population in the world, bypassing the US. This clearly shows that the primary home of the Jewish people today is no longer the US but Eretz Israel. One could say that the year 2001, the beginning of the 21st century, began another level of the paradigm shift in Aliyah this time from the West, which originally started 120 years ago from Russia, and has continued to grow in an unprecedented way from the USA.

Wall Street Falls

In September/October of 2008, the Lion again roared, this time over Wall Street and the economy of the USA. It is interesting that this book cover, which I designed in 1987, (the same cover for all 8 editions) has a picture of a man trying to break away from Wall Street, in essence the USA, is the exact reality the American Jews encounter today. May the Jewish people soon recognize the roar of the Lion and break free to Israel.

Less than two weeks after the stock market started falling, on October 10, 2008, the day after Yom Kippur (the Day of Atonement, the only day on the Jewish calendar when everything comes to a stand-still), again I was watching CNN in Nazareth, Israel on our annual Convocation and Watchmen's Tour of Israel. The stock market fell almost 2,000 points in 1.5 hours and approximately 7000 points in 3 weeks, one of the worst drops in History.

The Lion of Judah has been roaring over the economy in a way not seen in over 80 years, since the Great Depression of 1929. Many believe it could end up being much worse than the collapse of 1929 before it's over. Tens of millions of Americans' homes are in foreclosure due to buying houses way beyond their means. This has greatly affected the housing and building industries. The high-tech and automobile industries have been hit in a significant way: General Motors, Chrysler and many banks went bankrupt. The average American has approximately $15,000 in credit card debt, which has not yet factored into the current crisis; this has yet to surface. In the last months of 2008 alone, 3.5 million people lost their jobs in the USA and unemployment has grown by 8.5%. By July 2009, 6.5 million Americans lost their jobs, and 9.5% were unemployed, by November 2009 the Unemployment rate had risen to 10,2 %..

In his article from The Jerusalem Post, "The 30's Are Back: the US may be on track to 25% unemployment," Nitzan Cohen says, "On July 10th 2009, after 4 months of rallying, Wall Street returned from July 4th

Independence Day vacation 2009, in a gloomier mood, as indexes took a few steps back after weeks of optimistic reports that we had hit bottom. But the June job reports said, 460,000 Americans lost jobs in June alone. The unemployment rate does not include a broader unemployment rate called U-6, which includes people who stop looking for work or can't find full-time jobs. The realization that the economy seems to be in a far worse state than previously assumed is finally starting to come to the attention of the US leadership. Vice-President Joseph Biden, admitted in the first week of July 2009, that President Obama's administration had misread the economy and didn't fully understand the depth of the crisis, even as late as January 2009. Paul Krugman (Obama advisor) called for another massive bail-out plan on top of the 800 billion scheme that was approved just 4 months ago (March 2009). His pessimistic read on the current state of the economy is probably right. But we learned from the November Jobs Report, we are still getting very close to the frightening numbers seen in the 1930's." The national debt has doubled during the last 6 years to over 12 trillion dollars, an astronomical figure, which includes the Bush Administration.

The Health Insurance Plan for the USA which would help the poor could also rise the national debt trillions of more dollars.

It's time for Israelis in the USA and American Jews to invest in, return and make Aliyah to Israel, before greater economic shakings and judgments come upon the USA.

Ben Bernanke the Chairman of Federal Reserve received the Man of the Year award for 2009 for bringing the economy 12 trillion in debt. President Obama received the Nobel Peace Prize for overseeing Trillions of Dollars of indebtedness and hoping that there will be peace.

David Wilkerson, a New York City pastor, prophesied in his book, "America's Last Call: On the Brink of a Financial Holocaust" published in 1998: In the last year of President So-and-so's second term, on October 10th, G-d laid siege on the American economy and lifestyle..." That's just how precise G-d is in his judgments!" (pg. 23) It is interesting that on October 10th of President George W. Bush's last year of his 2-term presidency, Wall Street fell, as David Wilkerson said it would, almost 2000 points in 1.5 hours and 7,000 points within the following weeks. David Wilkerson has prophesied that the USA will experience great destruction and in the long-run become a third-world nation.

Invest in Israel for your future and be blessed
As of September 1st 2009, the Israeli economy and strength of the shekel is one of the highest in the world. Real Estate prices continue to rise in spite of the world economic crisis. Investing in real estate in Israel has proven to be a wise investment over the last decade and it appears that it will be in the future as well. It is especially recommended that Jews in the diaspora, many of whom will end up in Israel, invest now for their future. Seriously consider buying a home in Israel, as an investment but also as a way to prepare for your future. Prepare now for the paradigm-shift of Aliyah that is beginning from the West to Israel.

Aliyah is increasing from the West: Join the paradigm-shift to Israel
In addition to first time Aliyah, it is estimated that approximately 15,000 Israelis have returned to Israel since the market crash in October 2008, mostly from the USA. Orthodox and other Aliyah continues to increase from the USA through the efforts of Nefesh b' Nefesh, an organization committed to facilitating Aliyah from the USA and the UK Rabbi Yehoshua Fass, founder and executive director of Nefesh b' Nefesh, says, "While Aliyah is declining in other parts of the world, it is increasing from the USA and from the West." Through their education and support, 98% of the olim (Jewish immigrants to the land of Israel) are still in the land after 7 years, which is an amazing success rate. Rabbi Fass says, "Aliyah is now on the map in North America. It has come from the fringes to the mainstream. It was eccentric or unrealistic but today it is realistic and ideal." Through the combined efforts of Nefesh b' Nefesh and the Jewish Agency, the image of Aliyah has changed. With the newly elected head of the Jewish Agency, Natan Sharansky, a famous refusenik from Russia and Rabbi Fass, working together, we believe for a major breakthrough of Aliyah from the USA and the West in the coming decade. Rabbi Fass has joined every flight of the dozens of planeloads of new olim of Nefesh b' Nefesh in the last 8 years. He has been highly inspired to see tens of thousands of Jews making Aliyah to Israel from the USA and the West. Aliyah rose significantly to 17% in 2009 from the USA.

According to Rabbi Riskin, the chief Rabbi of Ephrat, Israel, a growing number of Orthodox families are making Aliyah from New York, as they can no longer afford to send their many children to private Jewish schools due to the downfall of the US economy, coupled with the benefit of free education in Israel. The Conservative Jewish Movement in America is now actively promoting Aliyah. Tzvi Graetz says they hope to at least double Aliyah from North America through their movement in the next 2-3 years. Aliyah from France has increased significantly from 2002-2008, driven by increased anti-Semitism. However it appears until now, Latin American Jews are responding more than North American Jews.

Pray for the secular Jews in the US and in the West to have a revelation of the G-d of Israel and His eternal covenant with righteousness and the land of Israel (Gen. 15). Pray that they will follow G-d's heart, evidenced in the 700 Scriptures calling them home to Israel. Why is there not yet massive Aliyah from the US and the West among the Orthodox and Bible-believing Jews, as they believe and supposedly obey the Torah? Rabbi Ohr Hachaim, noted: "There is no other joy than residing in the land of Israel."

The words of Joshua to the people of Israel in Deuteronomy 11:12, in the Egyptian desert 3000 years ago, are also for this time:

"How long will you be unwilling to possess the land that G-d has given you?"

Paraphrased from an article Michael Freud wrote in The Jerusalem Post: If the Orthodox Jews seek guidance from Scripture about what they put in their mouth (i.e. what kind of raisins they should eat), they should be at least equally concerned from Scripture about Aliyah, where G-d has called them to live and their inheritance, i.e. planting their feet in Eretz Israel.
Pray that G-d will strengthen Prime Minister Benjamin Netanyahu and all future prime ministers of Israel to stand for one united Jerusalem and Israel. Pray he/they will greatly encourage and facilitate Aliyah from the West and all nations. Pray that co-existence between Jews and Arabs will grow until we see Egypt, Israel and Assyria worshipping G-d together as a blessing in the midst of the earth. (Isaiah 19:23-25)
If the newly elected President Obama and the US courts keep championing the killing of unborn babies and homosexual rights/marriages, as well as trying to divide Jerusalem and giving away the land of Israel, trying to freeze Jewish settlements and pushing Jews out of Judea and Samaria (the

heartland of Israel) in attempt of establishing an Islamic Palestinian state in their place (Joel 3:2), we will see increasing judgment coming on the USA. Rising anti-Semitism coupled with an increasing financial meltdown in the USA will result in a growing Aliyah movement of hundreds of thousands, even millions of North American Jews back to Israel in the coming decades.

Aliyah means to return to Israel, to ascend to Jerusalem, to build up Zion. A major need for Israel is not only the coming home of new immigrants, especially from the West, but also the return of Israelis to Israel, a "second Aliyah" so to speak. Approximately 1 million Israelis live abroad, including many of the most educated, talented and professional people. The Israeli education system is at a low point. The Israeli population has doubled since 1973 but the number of university positions has dropped 20%. By 2019, 2,500 senior lecturers and teachers will retire with little time to absorb their replacements. Unless urgent measures are taken, the academic world in Israel will not be able to serve as an engine to propel Israel forward. Israel must learn from Nefesh b' Nefesh, success in Aliyah from the West, in finding a way for thousands of Israeli academia who are abroad to return, to make Aliyah again, to the Promised Land, as well as hundreds of thousands of Israelis abroad in other fields of expertise (in business, science, etc.). Many of the most educated and professional Israelis need to come home to take Israel to the next level. Israelis abroad already know the Hebrew language, culture and have the experience that can take new immigrants decades to learn, if ever. With the great shakings in the West, this is the kairos-opportune time to do whatever is necessary to encourage and facilitate the return second Aliyah of the Israelis back to their home. Pray that G-d will give Israel the wisdom to find the way to encourage and facilitate hundreds of thousands of Israelis to come back to their home and build up Zion, preparing the way for Messiah.

I am honored to have received an Israeli permanent residency in 2008, after serving in Jerusalem for the last twenty-two years. G-d brought me here for the purpose of standing with the G-d of Israel for His people and nation. I encourage ALL Israelis abroad to come home to fulfill their calling and destiny. If Israelis appreciate their heritage and the great investment made in their lives to enable them to serve G-d and their nation, it's time to put first things first. It's time to come home in order to help Israel fulfill her corporate calling and destiny - to be a light to the nations.

According to the Jerusalem Post, many US Jews under thirty-five years old feel a great apathy towards Israel. Of these, 57% say the annihilation of Israel would not be a personal tragedy for them. A much greater emphasis on the G-d of Israel, Aliyah, G-d's eternal covenant with Israel and prayer must be invested in the over 2.5 million American Jews under thirty-five. This is approximately 40% of the emerging generation of Jews thirty-five and under worldwide. Investing in this emerging generation, to help them come back to Israel and G-d, is one of the most important investments that can be made for the future of Israel.

Just after becoming the Director of the Jewish Agency, the Freedom Award recipient refusenik, Natan Sharansky, understanding the need to help the emerging generation make Aliyah, opened campus Aliyah fellowships on 20 major college campuses with large Jewish student populations across the USA. Marie Freuger, a student at Florida Atlantic University, who is spending a semester at Hebrew University in Jerusalem, will be a campus representative for Aliyah in Florida. She says she applied for the fellowship because she thinks it will help in her plans for making Aliyah, while also helping and inspiring others.

Libran Avisar says, "Many Jewish students are thinking of moving to Israel after college but have no one to turn to for information or support. The Aliyah Campus Fellowship will provide students the information and support they need and the opportunity to meet others also considering moving to Israel." In the winter (2010), students seriously interested in Aliyah, will travel to Israel to network with professionals and other new olim.

I believe that Israel should offer more special highly subsidized familiarization tours, possibly even free ones, for American Jews who have never been to Israel. Can you imagine if one million new American Jews visited Israel in the next 5 years? This alone would increase tourism 15%. If 2% of these decided to make Aliyah, it would more than double Aliyah each year and greatly increase the economy and demographics of Israel.

David Wilkerson says that the financial state of the USA will fall

to the ground. Whether this happens in 2009 or in the coming years or decade, remains to be seen. Regardless, we are clearly in a time of a major paradigm shift for the Jewish world that began 120 years ago. At that time there were about 20,000 Jews in Jerusalem. Today, over 400,000 Jews live in Jerusalem and 5.35 million Jews, approximately 45% of world Jewry live in Israel which is the largest Jewish nation in the world.
According to the Bible, Ezekiel 39:27,28:

"When I have brought them back from the nations and have gathered them from the countries of their enemies, I will show myself holy through them in the sight of many nations. Then they will know that I am the Lord their G-d, for though I sent them into exile among the nations, I will gather them to their own land, not leaving any behind."

This shift of Aliyah will not end until all Jews in the world are living back in Israel. The growth increased almost ten times from 1948 to 2008, from 600,000 to 5.35 million Jews living in Israel. Someone said, "If you would do the best with your life, find out what G-d is doing in your generation and totally throw yourself into it." The primary thing that G-d has been doing, is doing, and will continue to do among the Jewish people, for those that have eyes to see and ears to hear, is bringing His people back to their land, Eretz Israel, and back to their G-d to fulfill their G-d-given calling and destiny to be a light to the nations.

May G-d's chosen Jewish people in this emerging generation learn from the lessons of history and come home to Israel and not be doomed to repeat the mistakes, of six million Jews in the previous generation, when almost all Rabbis told them to stay in Europe, while the prophets were telling them to flee to Israel. May G-d provide true prophets, Jewish and Christian, true shepherds/rabbis for the Jewish people in these last days.

Even as G-d shook the former Soviet Union in the 1980's (the fall of communism) to bring home the Jews from the North, in a similar way He is beginning to shake and will continue to shake the USA until the Jews from the West come home. The biblical prophets, clearly stated in G-d's word, the Jewish Bible, the End-time covenantal promised land of blessing is not the USA, but Israel. Jewish people need to heed the two warnings:

1) the 9/11 terrorist attack on New York City and the USA of 2001
2) and the financial meltdown of 2008-2009.

The USA will never be the same again. Much greater shakings and judgments will come on the USA.

Jeremiah 30:11 says,

> **"Though I completely destroy all the nations where I have scattered you...I will not completely destroy Israel."**

This could be economic and/or nuclear destruction.

> **"Come out of her, My people, run for your lives, run from the fierce anger of the Lord." (Jeremiah 51:45)**

Jonah 2:8 says,

> **"Those who cling to worthless idols, forfeit the grace that will be theirs."**

When will the Jews hear and heed the roar and come trembling from the West?

Great shakings will continue until G-d's chosen covenant people come trembling from the West to their covenant homeland, Israel. The Lion is roaring louder and louder and great shakings will continue until His people come trembling to Israel from the West. When will the Jews hear the roar? When will they heed the roar? Every Jew in the world is called to Eretz Israel, according to the Bible. We pray that hundreds of thousands and millions will come in the coming decades. Eventually, all Jews who remain alive will end up in Israel. (Ezekiel 39:28)

Leave the West and invest in His Kingdom covenantal promise land before things worsen and you lose more, possibly everything, in the USA meltdown. Join in the progressive paradigm shift to Israel before it's too late. Come home to Israel, the most blessed land in the history of the world, the land of Abraham, Isaac, Jacob and King David, where the Son of David will reign on the throne of David in righteousness and justice now and forevermore, (Isaiah 9:7) Prepare the way for the greatest Kingdom ever, the coming restored Kingdom of Israel, which will be much greater and glorious than David and Solomon's kingdoms, where the King Lion of Judah will lay down with the lamb. (Isaiah 11) Hear the roar, heed the roar, break loose from the Babylon of American, pass through, pass through the gates to Jerusalem (Isaiah 62:10), prepare the way for the King of Glory (Psalm 24).

Shalom, welcome home to Jerusalem and Israel,

Tom Hess

YOU HAVE NOT FINISHED READING THIS BOOK UNTIL YOU HAVE READ THE SEVEN HUNDRED SCRIPTURE VERSES IN APPENDIX A!

Genesis 31:13 "I am the God of Bethel, where you anointed a pillar

Appendix A

Seven Hundred Verses of Scripture

To read, pray and meditate on!

Here are over 700 verses of scripture where God promises the Land of Canaan to His chosen people and commands or encourages them to return to the Land of Israel which He gave to them as an everlasting inheritance:

Genesis 12:1-3 (God's promise to Abraham and his descendants) The LORD had said to Abram, "Leave your country, your people and your father's household and go to the land I will show you. I will make you into a great nation and I will bless you; I will make your name great, and you will be a blessing. I will bless those who bless you, and whoever curses you I will curse; and all peoples on earth will be blessed through you."

Genesis 12:6-7 Abram traveled through the land as far as the site of the great tree of Moreh at Shechem. At that time the Canaanites were in the land. The LORD appeared to Abram and said, "To your offspring I will give this land."

Genesis 13:1-2 So Abram went up from Egypt to the Negev, with his wife and everything he had, and Lot went with him. Abram had become very wealthy in livestock and in silver and gold.

Genesis 13:14-17 The LORD said to Abram after Lot had parted from him, "Lift up your eyes from where you are and look north and south, east and west. All the land that you see I will give to you and your offspring forever. I will make your offspring like the dust of the earth, so that if anyone could count the dust, then your offspring could be counted. Go, walk through the length and breadth of the land, for I am giving it to you."

Genesis 15:7 He [God] also said to him, "I am the LORD, who brought you out of Ur of the Chaldeans to give you this land to take possession of it."

Genesis 15:13-14 Then the LORD said to him, "Know for certain that your descendants will be strangers in a country not their own, and they will be enslaved and mistreated four hundred years. But I will punish the nation they serve as slaves, and afterward they will come out with great possessions."

Genesis 15:18-21 On that day the LORD made a covenant with Abram and said, "To your descendants I give this land, from the river of Egypt to the great river, the Euphrates—the land of the Kenites, Kenizzites, Kadmonites, Hittites, Perizzites, Rephaites, Amorites, Canaanites, Girgashites and Jebusites."

Genesis 17:5-6 "No longer will you be called Abram, your name will be Abraham, for I have made you a father of many nations. I will make you very fruitful; I will make nations of you, and kings will come from you."

Genesis 17:7-8 "I will establish my covenant as an everlasting covenant between me and you and your descendants after you for the generations to come, to be your God and the God of your descendants after you. The whole land of Canaan, where you are now an alien, I will give as an everlasting possession to you and your descendants after you; and I will be their God."

Genesis 17:19 Then God said, "Yes, but your wife Sarah will bear you a son and you will call him Isaac. I will establish my covenant with him as an everlasting covenant for his descendants after him."

Genesis 18:18-19 "Abraham will surely become a great and powerful nation, and all nations on earth will be blessed through him. For I have chosen him, so that he will direct his children and his household after him to keep the way of the LORD by doing what is right and just, so that the LORD will bring about for Abraham what he has promised him."

Genesis 22:17-18 "I will surely bless you and make your descendants as numerous as the stars in the sky and as the sand on the seashore. Your descendants will take possession of the cities of their enemies, and through your offspring all nations on earth will be blessed, because you have obeyed me."

Genesis 23:17 (Purchase of Cave of Machpelah—burial site of Patriarchs)

Genesis 25:7-11 (Burial of Abraham in Cave of Machpelah—Hebron)

Genesis 26:3-4 "Stay in this land for a while, and I will be with you and will bless you. For to you and your descendants I will give all these lands and will confirm the oath I swore to your father Abraham. I will make your descendants as numerous as the stars in the sky and will give them all these lands, and through your offspring all nations on earth will be blessed."

Genesis 26:12 Isaac planted crops in that land and the same year reaped a hundredfold, because the LORD blessed him.

Genesis 26:24 That night the LORD appeared to him and said, "I am the God of your father Abraham. Do not be afraid, for I am with you; I will bless you and will increase the number of your descendants for the sake of my servant Abraham."

Genesis 28:3-4 "May God Almighty bless you and make you fruitful and increase your numbers until you become a community of peoples. May he give you and your descendants the blessing given to Abraham, so that you may take possession of the land where you now live as an alien, the land God gave to Abraham."

Genesis 28:13-15 There above it stood the LORD, and he said: "I am the LORD, the God of your father Abraham and the God of Isaac. I will give you and your descendants the land on which you are lying. Your descendants will be like the dust of the earth, and you will spread out to the west and to the east, to the north and to the south. All peoples on earth will be blessed through you and your offspring. I am with you and will watch over you wherever you go, and I will bring you back to this land. I will not leave you until I have done what I have promised you."

Genesis 31:3 Then the LORD said to Jacob, "Go back to the land of your fathers and to your relatives, and I will be with you."

and where you made a vow to me. Now leave this land at once and go back to your native land."

Genesis 31:17 Then Jacob put his children and his wives on camels and he drove all his livestock ahead of him, along with all the goods he had accumulated in Paddan Abram, to go to his father Isaac in the land of Canaan.

Genesis 32:9-10 Then Jacob prayed, "O G-d of my father Abraham, G-d of my father Isaac, O LORD, who said to me, 'Go back to your country and your relatives, and I will make you prosper,' I am unworthy of all the kindness and faithfulness you have shown your servant."

Genesis 35:10-13 G-d said to him, "Your name is Jacob, but you will no longer be called Jacob; your name will be Israel." So he named him Israel. And G-d said to him, "I am G-d Almighty; be fruitful and increase in number. A nation and a community of nations will come from you, and kings will come from your body. The land I gave to Abraham and Isaac I also give to you, and I will give this land to your descendants after you."

Genesis 35:27-29 (Isaac buried by Esau and Jacob in the Promised Land)

Genesis 46:3-4 "I am G-d, the G-d of your father," he said. "Do not be afraid to go down to Egypt, for I will make you into a great nation there. I will go down to Egypt with you, and I will surely bring you back again. And Joseph's own hand will close your eyes."

Genesis 48:21 Then Israel [Jacob] said to Joseph, "I am about to die, but G-d will be with you and take you back to the land of your fathers."

Genesis 49:29-32 (Death of Jacob—Israel—and burial in the promised land) Then he gave them these instructions: "I am about to be gathered to my people. Bury me with my fathers in the cave in the field of Ephron the Hittite, the cave in the field of Machpelah, near Mamre in Canaan, which Abraham bought as a burial place from Ephron the Hittite, along with the field. There Abraham and his wife Sarah were buried, there Isaac and his wife Rebekah were buried, and there I buried Leah. The field and the cave in it were bought from the Hittites."

Genesis 50:12-14 (Burial in Canaan) So Jacob's sons did as he had commanded them: They carried him to the land of Canaan and buried him in the cave in the field of Machpelah, near Mamre, which Abraham had bought as a burial place from Ephron the Hittite, along with the field. After burying his father, Joseph returned to Egypt, together with his brothers and all the others who had gone with him to bury his father.

Genesis 50:24-25 Then Joseph said to his brothers, "I am about to die. But G-d will surely come to your aid and take you up out of this land to the land he promised on oath to Abraham, Isaac and Jacob." And Joseph made the sons of Israel swear an oath and said, "G-d will surely come to your aid, and then you must carry my bones up from this place."

Exodus 1:1-5 (70 descendants of Jacob go down to Egypt to escape famine. About 430 years later, in Exodus 12:37-38, 3,000,000 Jewish people are brought out of Egypt to return to the land G-d promised them.)

Exodus 2:24 G-d heard their groaning and He remembered His covenant with Abraham, with Isaac and with Jacob.

Exodus 3:7-8 The LORD said, "I have indeed seen the misery of my people in Egypt. I have heard them crying out because of their slave drivers, and I am concerned about their suffering. So I have come down to rescue them from the hand of the Egyptians and to bring them up out of that land into a good and spacious land, a land flowing with milk and honey."

Exodus 6:8 And I will bring you to the land I swore with uplifted hand to give to Abraham, to Isaac and to Jacob. I will give it to you as a possession. I am the LORD.

Exodus 12:24-25 (The Passover) "Obey these instructions as a lasting ordinance for you and your descendants. When you enter the land that the LORD will give you as he promised, observe this ceremony."

Exodus 12:35-36 (Taking the wealth out of Egypt) The Israelites did as Moses instructed and asked the Egyptians for articles of silver and gold and for clothing. The LORD had made the Egyptians favorably disposed toward the people, and they gave them what they asked for; so they plundered the Egyptians.

Exodus 13:5 "When the LORD brings you into the land of the

Canaanites, Hittites, Amorites, Hivites and Jebusites—the land he swore to your forefathers to give you, a land flowing with milk and honey— you are to observe this ceremony in this month."

Exodus 13:11-12 "After the LORD brings you into the land of the Canaanites and gives it to you, as he promised on oath to you and your forefathers, you are to give over to the LORD the first offspring of every womb. All the first born males of your livestock belong to the LORD."

Exodus 19:5 'Now if you obey me fully and keep my covenant, then out of all nations you will be my treasured possession.'

Exodus 20:2 "I am the LORD your G-d, who brought you out of Egypt, out of the land of slavery."

Exodus 23:20-23 "See, I am sending an angel ahead of you to guard you along the way and to bring you to the place I have prepared. Pay attention to him and listen to what he says. Do not rebel against him; he will not forgive your rebellion, since my Name is in him. If you listen carefully to what he says and do all that I say, I will be an enemy to your enemies and will oppose those who oppose you. My angel will go ahead of you and bring you into the land of the Amorites, Hittites, Perizzites, Canaanites, Hivites and Jebusites, and I will wipe them out."

Exodus 23:31 "I will establish your borders from the Red Sea to the Sea of the Philistines, and from the desert to the River. I will hand over to you the people who live in the land and you will drive them out before you."

Exodus 29:45-46 "Then I will dwell among the Israelites and be their G-d. They will know that I am the LORD their G-d, who brought them out of Egypt so that I might dwell among them. I am the LORD their G-d."

Exodus 32:13 "Remember your servants Abraham, Isaac and Israel, to whom you swore by your own self: 'I will make your descendants as numerous as the stars in the sky and I will give your descendants all this land I promised them, and it will be their inheritance forever.'"

Exodus 33:1 Then the LORD said to Moses, "Leave this place, you and the people you brought up out of Egypt, and go up to the land I promised on oath to Abraham, Isaac and Jacob, saying 'I will give it to your descendants.'"

Exodus 34:24 "I will drive out nations before you and enlarge your territory, and no one will covet your land when you go up three times each year to appear before the LORD your G-d."

Leviticus 20:24 "But I said to you, 'You will possess their land; I will give it to you as an inheritance, a land flowing with milk and honey.' I am the LORD your G-d, who has set you apart from the nations."

Leviticus 25:1-2 The LORD said to Moses on Mt. Sinai, "Speak to the Israelites and say to them: 'When you enter the land I am going to give you, the land itself must observe a Sabbath to the LORD.'"

Leviticus 25:10-13 (Year of Jubilee) Consecrate the fiftieth year and proclaim liberty throughout the land to all its inhabitants. It shall be a jubilee for you; each one of you is to return to his family property and each to his own clan.... In this Year of Jubilee everyone is to return to his own property.

Leviticus 25:18-19 "Follow my decrees and be careful to obey my laws, and you will live safely in the land. Then the land will yield its fruit, and you will eat your fill and live there in safety."

Leviticus 25:38 "I am the LORD your G-d, who brought you out of Egypt to give you the land of Canaan and to be your G-d."

Leviticus 25:41 Then he and his children are to be released, and he will go back to his own clan and to the property of his forefathers.

Leviticus 26:9 I will look on you with favor and make you fruitful and increase your numbers, and I will keep my covenant with you.

Leviticus 26:42 I will remember my covenant with Jacob and my covenant with Isaac and my covenant with Abraham, and I will remember the land.

Numbers 10:29 Now Moses said to Hobab son of Reuel the

Midianite, Moses' father-in-law, "We are setting out for the place about which the LORD said, 'I will give it to you.' Come with us and we will treat you well, for the LORD has promised good things to Israel."

Numbers 11:12 (Moses speaking to G-d) "Did I conceive all these people? Did I give them birth? Why do you tell me to carry them in my arms, as a nurse carries an infant, to the land you promised on oath to their forefathers?"

Numbers 13:1-2 The LORD said to Moses, "Send some men to explore the land of Canaan, which I am giving to the Israelites. From each ancestral tribe send one of its leaders."

Numbers 13:17-20 When Moses sent them to explore Canaan, he said, "Go up through the Negev and on into the hill country. See what the land is like and whether the people who live there are strong or weak, few or many. What kind of land do they live in? Is it good or bad? What kind of towns do they live in? Are they unwalled or fortified? How is the soil? Is it fertile or poor? Are there trees on it or not? Do your best to bring back some of the fruit of the land."

Numbers 14:8 If the LORD is pleased with us, he will lead us into that land, a land flowing with milk and honey, and will give it to us.

Numbers 15:17-19 The LORD said to Moses, "Speak to the Israelites and say to them: 'When you enter the land to which I am taking you and you eat the food of the land, present a portion as an offering to the LORD.'"

Numbers 26:52-56 The LORD said to Moses, "The land is to be allotted to them as an inheritance based on the number of names. To a larger group give a larger inheritance, and to a smaller group a smaller one; each is to receive its inheritance according to the number of those listed. Be sure that the land is distributed by lot. What each group inherits will be according to the names for its ancestral tribe. Each inheritance is to be distributed by lot among the larger and smaller groups."

Numbers 27:12 Then the LORD said to Moses, "Go up this mountain in the Abarim range and see the land I have given the Israelites."

Numbers 32:7 Why do you discourage the Israelites from going over into the land the LORD has given them?

Numbers 32:22 Then when the land is subdued before the LORD, you may return and be free from your obligation to the LORD and to Israel. And this land will be your possession before the LORD.

Numbers 33:51-54 Speak to the Israelites and say to them: "When you cross the Jordan into Canaan, drive out all the inhabitants of the land before you. Destroy all their carved images and their cast idols, and demolish all their high places. Take possession of the land and settle in it, for I have given you the land to possess. Distribute the land by lot, according to your clans. To a larger group give a larger inheritance, and to a smaller group a smaller one. Whatever falls to them by lot will be theirs. Distribute it according to your ancestral tribes."

Numbers 34 (Boundaries of Canaan)

Numbers 36:7-9 No inheritance in Israel is to pass from tribe to tribe, for every Israelite shall keep the tribal land inherited from his forefathers. Every daughter who inherits land in any Israelite tribe must marry someone in her father's tribal clan, so that every Israelite will possess the inheritance of his fathers. No inheritance may pass from tribe to tribe, for each Israelite tribe is to keep the land it inherits.

Deuteronomy 1:8 See, I have given you this land. Go in and take possession of the land that the LORD swore he would give to your fathers— to Abraham, Isaac and Jacob—and to their descendants after them.

Deuteronomy 1:21 See, the LORD your G-d has given you the land. Go up and take possession of it as the LORD, the G-d of your fathers, told you. Do not be afraid; do not be discouraged.

Deuteronomy 1:25 Taking with them some of the fruit of the land, they brought it down to us and reported, "It is a good land that the LORD our G-d is giving us."

Deuteronomy 1:38-39 But your assistant, Joshua son of Nun, will enter it. Encourage him, because he will lead Israel to inherit it. And the little ones that you said would be taken captive, your children who do not yet know good from bad—they will enter the land. I will give it to them and they will take possession of it.

Deuteronomy 3:28   But commission Joshua, and encourage and strengthen him, for he will lead this people across and will cause them to inherit the land that you will see.

Deuteronomy 4:1   Hear now, O Israel, the decrees and laws I am about to teach you. Follow them so that you may live and may go in and take possession of the land that the LORD, the G-d of your fathers, is giving you.

Deuteronomy 4:5-6   See, I have taught you decrees and laws as the LORD my G-d commanded me, so that you may follow them in the land you are entering to take possession of it. Observe them carefully, for this will show your wisdom and understanding to the nations, who will hear about all these decrees and say, "Surely this great nation is a wise and understanding people."

Deuteronomy 4:14   And the LORD directed me at that time to teach you the decrees and laws you are to follow in the land that you are crossing the Jordan to possess.

Deuteronomy 4:22-24   I will die in this land; I will not cross the Jordan; but you are about to cross over and take possession of that good land. Be careful not to forget the covenant of the LORD your G-d that he made with you; do not make for yourselves an idol in the form of anything the LORD your G-d has forbidden.

Deuteronomy 4:27-31   The LORD will scatter you among the peoples, and only a few of you will survive among the nations to which the LORD will drive you. There you will worship manmade G-ds of wood and stone, which cannot see or hear or eat or smell. But if from there you seek the LORD your G-d, you will find him if you look for him with all your heart and with all your soul. When you are in distress and all these things have happened to you, then in later days you will return to the LORD your G-d and obey him. For the LORD your G-d is a merciful G-d; he will not abandon or destroy you or forget the covenant with your forefathers, which he confirmed to them by oath.

Deuteronomy 4:32-38   Ask now about the former days, long before your time, from the day G-d created man on the earth; ask from one end of the heavens to the other. Has anything so great as this ever happened, or has anything like it ever been heard of? Has any other people heard the voice of G-d speaking out of fire, as you have, and lived? Has any G-d ever tried to take for himself one nation out of another nation, by testings, by miraculous signs and wonders, by war, by a mighty hand and an outstretched arm, or by great and awesome deeds, like all the things the LORD your G-d did for you in Egypt before your very eyes? You were shown these things so that you might know that the LORD is G-d; besides him there is no other. From heaven he made you hear his voice to discipline you. On earth he showed you his great fire, and you heard his words from out of the fire. Because he loved your forefathers and chose their descendants after them, he brought you out of Egypt by his Presence and his great strength, to drive out before you nations greater and stronger than you and to bring you into their land to give it to you for your inheritance, as it is today.

Deuteronomy 4:39-40 Acknowledge and take to heart this day that the LORD is G-d in heaven above and on the earth below. There is no other. Keep his decrees and commands, which I am giving you today, so that it may go well with you and your children after you and that you may live long in the land the LORD your G-d gives you for all time.

Deuteronomy 5:32-33 So be careful to do what the LORD your G-d has commanded you; do not turn aside to the right or to the left. Walk in all the way that the LORD your G-d has commanded you, so that you may live and prosper and prolong your days in the land that you will possess.

Deuteronomy 6:3 Hear, O Israel, and be careful to obey so that it may go well with you and that you may increase greatly in a land flowing with milk and honey, just as the LORD, the G-d of your fathers, promised you.

Deuteronomy 6:10-12 When the LORD your G-d brings you into the land he swore to your fathers, to Abraham, Isaac and Jacob, to give you—a land with large, flourishing cities you did not build, houses filled with all kinds of good things you did not provide, wells you did not dig, and vineyards and olive groves you did not plant—then when you eat and are satisfied, be careful that you do not forget the LORD, who brought you out of Egypt, out of the land of slavery.

Deuteronomy 6:18 Do what is right and good in the LORD'S sight, so that it may go well with you and you may go in and take over the good land that the LORD promised on oath to your forefathers.

Deuteronomy 6:23 But he brought us out from there to bring us in and give us the land that he promised on oath to our forefathers.

Deuteronomy 7:7-9 The LORD did not set his affection on you and choose you because you were more numerous than other peoples, for you were the fewest of all peoples. But it was because the LORD loved you and kept the oath he swore to your forefathers that he brought you out with a mighty hand and redeemed you from the land of slavery, from the power of Pharaoh king of Egypt. Know therefore that the LORD your G-d is G-d; he is the faithful G-d, keeping his covenant of love to a thousand generations of those who love him and keep his commands.

Deuteronomy 7:12-13 If you pay attention to these laws and are careful to follow them then the LORD your G-d will keep his covenant of love with you, as he swore to your forefathers. He will love you and bless you and increase your numbers. He will bless the fruit of your womb, the crops of your land—your grain, new wine and oil—the calves of your herds and the lambs of your flocks in the land that he swore to your forefathers to give you.

Deuteronomy 8:1 Be careful to follow every command I am giving you today, so that you may live and increase and may enter and possess the land that the LORD promised on oath to your forefathers.

Deuteronomy 8:6-9 Observe the commands of the LORD your G-d, walking in his ways and revering him. For the LORD your G-d is bringing you into a good land—a land with streams and pools of water, with springs flowing in the valleys and hills; a land with wheat and barley, vines and fig trees, pomegranates, olive oil and honey; a land where bread will not be scarce and you will lack nothing; a land where the rocks are iron and you can dig copper out of the hills.

Deuteronomy 8:10 When you have eaten and are satisfied, praise the LORD your G-d for the good land he has given you.

Deuteronomy 8:18 But remember the LORD your G-d, for it is he who gives you the ability to produce wealth, and so confirms his covenant, which he swore to your forefathers, as it is today.

Deuteronomy 9:1 Hear, O Israel. You are now about to cross the Jordan to go in and dispossess nations greater and stronger than you, with large cities that have walls up to the sky.

Deuteronomy 9:5 It is not because of your righteousness or your integrity that you are going in to take possession of their land; but on account of the wickedness of these nations.

Deuteronomy 10:11 "Go," the LORD said to me, "and lead the people on their way, so that they may enter and possess the land that I swore to their fathers to give them."

Deuteronomy 11:8-9 Observe therefore all the commands I am giving you today, so that you may have the strength to go in and take over the land that you are crossing the Jordan to possess, and so that you may live long in the land that the LORD swore to your forefathers to give to them and their descendants, a land flowing with milk and honey.

Deuteronomy 11:10-12 The land you are entering to take over is not like the land of Egypt, from which you have come, where you planted your seed and irrigated it by foot as in a vegetable garden. But the land you are crossing the Jordan to take possession of is a land of mountains and valleys that drinks rain from heaven. It is a land the LORD your G-d cares for; the eyes of the LORD your G-d are continually on it from the beginning of the year to its end.

Deuteronomy 11:18-21 Fix these words of mine in your hearts and minds; tie them as symbols on your hands and bind them on your foreheads. Teach them to your children, talking about them when you sit at home and when you walk along the road, when you lie down and when you get up. Write them on the doorframes of your houses and on your gates, so that your days and the days of your children may be many in the land that the LORD swore to give your forefathers, as many as the days that the heavens are above the earth.

Deuteronomy 11:24 Every place where you set your foot will be yours; your territory will extend from the desert to Lebanon, and from the Euphrates River to the western sea.

Deuteronomy 11:31-32 You are about to cross the Jordan to enter and take possession of the land the LORD your G-d is giving you. When you have taken it over and are living there, be sure that you obey all the decrees and laws I am setting before you today.

Deuteronomy 15:4-6 However, there should be no poor among you, for in the land the LORD your G-d is giving you to possess as your inheritance, he will richly bless you, if only you fully obey the LORD your G-d and are careful to follow all these commands I am giving you today. For the LORD your G-d will bless you as he has promised, and you will lend to many nations but will borrow from none. You will rule over many nations but none will rule over you.

Deuteronomy 16:20 Follow justice and justice alone, so that you may live and possess the land the LORD your G-d is giving you.

Deuteronomy 17:14-15 When you enter the land the LORD your G-d is giving you and have taken possession of it and settled in it, and you say, "Let us set a king over us like all the nations around us," be sure to appoint over you the king the LORD your G-d chooses. He must be from among your own brothers. Do not place a foreigner over you, one who is not a brother Israelite.

Deuteronomy 18:9 When you enter the land the LORD your G-d is giving you, do not learn to imitate the detestable ways of the nations there.

Deuteronomy 26:1-3 When you have entered the land the LORD your G-d is giving you as an inheritance and have taken possession of it and settled in it, take some of the first-fruits of all that you produce from the soil of the land the LORD your G-d is giving you and put them in a basket. Then go to the place the LORD your G-d will choose as a dwelling for his Name and say to the priest in office at the time, "I declare today to the LORD your G-d that I have come to the land the LORD swore to our forefathers to give us."

Deuteronomy 26:15 Look down from heaven, your holy dwelling place, and bless your people Israel and the land you have given us as you promised an oath to our forefathers, a land flowing with milk and honey.

Deuteronomy 26:18-19 And the LORD has declared this day that you are his people, his treasured possession as he promised, and that you are to keep all his commands. He has declared that he will set you in praise, fame and honor high above all the nations he has made and that you will be a people holy to the LORD your G-d, as he promised.

Deuteronomy 27:3 Write on them all the words of this law when you have crossed over to enter the land the LORD your G-d is giving you, a land flowing with milk and honey, just as the LORD, the G-d of your fathers, promised you.

Deuteronomy 28:8 The LORD will send a blessing on your barns and on everything you put your hand to. The LORD your G-d will bless you in the land he is giving you.

Deuteronomy 28:9-11 The LORD will establish you as his holy people, as he promised you on oath, if you keep the commands of the LORD your G-d and walk in his ways. Then all the peoples on earth will see that you are called by the name of the LORD, and they will fear you. The LORD will grant you abundant prosperity—in the fruit of your womb, the young of your livestock and the crops of your ground—in the land he swore to your forefathers to give you.

Deuteronomy 30:1-5 When all these blessings and curses I have set before you come upon you and you take them to heart wherever the LORD your G-d disperses you among the nations, and when you and your children return to the LORD your G-d and obey him with all your heart and with all your soul according to everything I command you today, then the LORD your G-d will restore your fortunes and have compassion on you and gather you again from all the nations where he scattered you. Even if you have been banished to the most distant land under the heavens, from there the LORD your G-d will gather you and bring you back. He will bring you to the land that belonged to your fathers, and you will take possession of it. He will make you more prosperous and numerous than your fathers.

Deuteronomy 30:19-20 This day I call heaven and earth as witnesses against you that I have set before you life and death, blessings and curses. Now choose life, so that you and your children may live and that you may love the LORD your G-d, listen to his voice, and hold fast to him. For the LORD is your life, and he will give you many years in the land he swore to give to your fathers, Abraham, Isaac and Jacob.

Deuteronomy 31:3 The LORD your G-d himself will cross over ahead of you. He will destroy these nations before you, and you will take possession of their land. Joshua also will cross over ahead of you, as the LORD said.

Deuteronomy 31:7 Then Moses summoned Joshua and said to him in the presence of all Israel, "Be strong and courageous, for you must go with this people into the land that the LORD swore to their forefathers to give them, and you must divide it among them as their inheritance."

Deuteronomy 31:19-22 "Now write down for yourselves this song and teach it to the Israelites and have them sing it, so that it may be a witness for me against them. When I have brought them into the land flowing with milk and honey, the land I promised on oath to their forefathers, and when they eat their fill and thrive, they will turn to other G-ds and worship them, rejecting me and breaking my covenant. And when many disasters and difficulties come upon them, this song will testify against them, because it will not be forgotten by their descendants. I know what they are disposed to do, even before I bring them into the land I promised them on oath." So Moses wrote down this song that day and taught it to the Israelites.

Deuteronomy 31:23 The LORD gave this command to Joshua son of Nun: "Be strong and courageous, for you will bring the Israelites into the land I promised them on oath, and I myself will be with you."

Deuteronomy 32:45-47 When Moses finished reciting all these words to all Israel, he said to them, "Take to heart all the words I have solemnly declared to you this day, so that you may command your children to obey carefully all the words of this law. They are not just idle words for you—they are your life. By them you will live long in the land you are crossing the Jordan to possess.

Deuteronomy 32:48-49 On that same day the LORD told Moses, "Go up into the Abarim Range to Mount Nebo in Moab, across from Jericho, and view Canaan, the land I am giving the Israelites as their own possession."

Deuteronomy 34:1-4 Then Moses climbed Mount Nebo from the plains of Moab to the top of Pisgah, across from Jericho. There the LORD showed him the whole land—from Gilead to Dan, all of Naphtali, the territory of Ephraim and Manasseh, all the land of Judah as far as the western sea, the Negev and the whole region from the valley of Jericho, the City of Palms, as far as Zoar. Then the LORD said to him, "This is the land I promised on oath to Abraham, Isaac and Jacob when I said, 'I will give it to your descendants.' I have let you see it with your eyes, but you will not cross over into it.'"

Joshua 1:2-6 Moses my servant is dead. Now then, you and all these people, get ready to cross the Jordan River into the land I am about to give to them—to the Israelites. I will give you every place where you set your foot, as I promised Moses. Your territory will extend from the desert to Lebanon, and from the great river, the Euphrates—all the Hittite country— to the Great Sea on the west. No one will be able to stand up against you all the days of your life. As I was with Moses, so I will be with you; I will never leave you nor forsake you. Be strong and courageous, because you will lead these people to inherit the land I swore to their forefathers to give them.

Joshua 1:15 Until the LORD gives them rest, as he has done for you, and until they too have taken possession of the land that the LORD your G-d is giving them.

Joshua 2:24 They said to Joshua, "The LORD has surely given the whole land into our hands; all the people are melting in fear because of us."

Joshua 5:10-12 On the evening of the fourteenth day of the month, while camped at Gilgal on the plains of Jericho, the Israelites celebrated the Passover. The day after the Passover, that very day, they ate some of the produce of the land: unleavened bread and roasted grain. The manna stopped the day after they ate this food from the land; there was no longer any manna for the Israelites, but that year they ate of the produce of Canaan.

Joshua 11:16-17 So Joshua took this entire land: the hill country, all the Negev, the whole region of Goshen, the western foothills, the Arabah and the mountains of Israel with their foothills, from Mount Halak, which rises toward Seir, to Baal Gad in the Valley of Lebanon below Mount Hermon. He captured all their kings and struck them down, putting them to death.

Joshua 11:23 So Joshua took the entire land, just as the LORD had directed Moses, and he gave it as an inheritance to Israel according to their tribal division. Then the land had rest from war.

Joshua 14:13-14 Then Joshua blessed Caleb son of Jephunneh and gave him Hebron as his inheritance. So Hebron has belonged to Caleb son of Jephunneh the Kennizzite ever since, because he followed the LORD, the G-d of Israel, wholeheartedly.

Joshua 13-19 (Describes the allocation of territories to the tribes of Israel.)

Joshua 22:4 Now that the LORD your G-d has given your brothers rest as he promised, return to your homes in the land that Moses the servant of the LORD gave you on the other side of the Jordan.

Joshua 22:7-8 When Joshua sent them home, he blessed them, saying, "Return to your homes with your great wealth—with large herds of livestock, with silver, gold, bronze and iron, and a great quantity of clothing—and divide with your brothers the plunder from your enemies."

Joshua 24:13 So I gave you a land on which you did not toil and cities you did not build; and you live in them and eat from vineyards and olive groves that you did not plant.

Joshua 24:29,32 (Joseph buried in the promised land with rest of Patriarchs)

Judges 1:1-2 After the death of Joshua, the Israelites asked the LORD, "Who will be the first to go up and fight for us against the Canaanites?" The LORD answered, "Judah is to go; I have given the land into their hands."

Judges 2:1 The Angel of the LORD went up from Gilgal to Bokim and said, "I brought you up out of Egypt and led you into the land that I swore to give to your forefathers. I said, 'I will never break my covenant with you.'"

Ruth 1:7 With her two daughters-in-law she left the place where she had been living and set out on the road that would take them back to the land of Judah.

I Samuel 22:5 But the prophet Gad said to David, "Do not stay in the stronghold. Go into the land of Judah."

II Samuel 7:10 And I will provide a place for my people Israel and will plant them so that they can have a home of their own and no longer be disturbed. Wicked people will not oppress them anymore, as they did at the beginning.

II Chronicles 30:9 If you return to the LORD, then your brothers and your children will be shown compassion by their captors and will come back to this land, for the LORD your G-d is gracious and compassionate. He will not turn His face from you if you return to him.

Ezra 10:7 A proclamation was then issued throughout Judah and Jerusalem for all the exiles to assemble in Jerusalem.

Ezra 8 (Return to Jerusalem from Babylonian captivity and bringing the wealth back to Jerusalem.)

Nehemiah 1:8-9 Remember the instruction you gave your servant Moses, saying, "If you are unfaithful, I will scatter you among the nations, but if you return to me and obey my commands, then even if your exiled people are at the farthest horizon, I will gather them from there and bring them to the place I have chosen as a dwelling for my Name."

Nehemiah 7 (The list of exiles who returned from the Babylonian Captivity.)

Nehemiah 7:66-67 The whole company numbered 42,360, besides their 7,337 menservants and maidservants; and they also had 245 men and women singers.

Nehemiah 9:7-8 You are the LORD G-d, who chose Abram and brought him out of Ur of the [] and named him Abraham. You found his heart faithful to you, and you made a covenant with him to give to his descendants the land of the Canaanites, Hittites, Amorites, Perizzites, Jebusites and Girgashites. You have kept your promise because you are righteous.

Nehemiah 9:23-25 You made their sons as numerous as the stars in the sky, and you brought them into the land that you told their fathers to enter and possess. Their sons went in and took possession of the land. You subdued before them the Canaanites, who lived in the land; you handed the Canaanites over to them, along with their kings and the peoples of the land, to deal with them as they pleased. They captured fortified cities and fertile land; they took possession of houses filled with all kinds of good things, wells already dug, vineyards, olive groves and fruit trees in abundance. They ate to the full and were well nourished; they reveled in your great goodness.

Psalm 2:8 Ask of me, and I will make the nations your inheritance, the ends of the earth your possession.

Psalm 14:7 Oh, that salvation for Israel would come out of Zion! When the LORD restores the fortunes of his people, let Jacob rejoice and Israel be glad!

Psalm 25:13 He will spend his days in prosperity, and his descendants will inherit the land.

Psalm 27:4 One thing I ask of the LORD, this is what I seek: that I may dwell in the house of the LORD all the days of my life, to gaze upon the beauty of the LORD and to seek him in his temple.

Psalm 33:12 Blessed is the nation whose G-d is the LORD, the people he chose for his inheritance.

Psalm 37:3 Trust in the LORD and do good; dwell in the land and enjoy safe pasture.

Psalm 37:11 But the meek will inherit the land and enjoy great peace.

Psalm 37:22 Those the LORD blesses will inherit the land, but those he curses will be cut off.

Psalm 37:29 The righteous will inherit the land and dwell in it forever.

Psalm 37:34 Wait for the LORD and keep his way. He will exalt you to inherit the land; when the wicked are cut off, you will see it.

Psalm 53:6 Oh, that salvation for Israel would come out of Zion! When G-d restores the fortunes of his people, let Jacob rejoice and Israel be glad!

Psalm 69:33-36 The LORD hears the needy and does not despise his captive people. Let heaven and earth praise him, the seas and all that move in them, for G-d will save Zion and rebuild the cities of Judah. Then people will settle there and possess it; the children of his servants will inherit it, and those who love his name will dwell there.

Psalm 74:2 Remember the people you purchased of old, the tribe of your inheritance, whom you redeemed—Mount Zion, where you dwelt.

Psalm 77:14-15 You are the G-d who performs miracles; you display your power among the peoples. With your mighty arm you redeemed your people, the descendants of Jacob and Joseph.

Psalm 78:54-55 Thus he brought them to the border of his holy land, to the hill country his right hand had taken. He drove out nations before them and allotted their lands to them as an inheritance; he settled the tribes of Israel in their homes.

Psalm 84:10 Better is one day in your courts than a thousand elsewhere; I would rather be a doorkeeper in the house of my G-d than dwell in the tents of the wicked.

Psalm 85:1 You showed favor to your land, O LORD; you restored the fortunes of Jacob.

Psalm 85:12 The LORD will indeed give what is good, and our land will yield its harvest.

Psalm 87:1-2 He has set his foundation on the holy mountain; the

LORD loves the gates of Zion more than all the dwellings of Jacob.

Psalm 94:14 For the LORD will not reject his people; he will never forsake his inheritance.

Psalm 105:6-11 O descendants of Abraham his servant, O sons of Jacob, his chosen ones. He is the LORD our G-d; his judgements are in all the earth. He remembers his covenant forever, the word he commanded, for a thousand generations, the covenant he made with Abraham, the oath he swore to Isaac. He confirmed it to Jacob as a decree, to Israel as an everlasting covenant: "To you I will give the land of Canaan as the portion you will inherit."

Psalm 105:37 He brought out Israel, laden with silver and gold, and from among their tribes no one faltered.

Psalm 105:42-45 For he remembered his holy promise given to his servant Abraham. He brought out his people with rejoicing, his chosen ones with shouts of joy; he gave them the lands of the nations, and they fell heir to what others had toiled for—that they might keep his precepts and observe his laws. Praise the LORD!

Psalm 106:47 Save us, O LORD our G-d, and gather us from the nations, that we may give thanks to your holy name and glory in your praise.

Psalm 107:2-3 Let the redeemed of the LORD say this—those he redeemed from the hand of the foe, those he gathered from the lands, from east and west, from north and south.

Psalm 107:7 He led them by a straight way to a city where they could settle.

Psalm 107:36-38 There he brought the hungry to live, and they founded a city where they could settle. They sowed fields and planted vineyards that yielded a fruitful harvest; he blessed them, and their numbers greatly increased, and he did not let their herds diminish.

Psalm 111:5-6 He provides food for those who fear him; he remembers his covenant forever. He has shown his people the power of his works, giving them the lands of other nations.

Psalm 114:1-2 When Israel came out of Egypt, the house of Jacob from a people of foreign tongue, Judah became G-d's sanctuary, Israel his dominion.

Psalm 121:4 Indeed, he who watches over Israel will neither slumber nor sleep.

Psalm 122:1-4 I rejoiced with those who said to me, "Let us go to the house of the LORD." Our feet are standing in your gates, O Jerusalem. Jerusalem is built like a city that is closely compacted together. That is where the tribes go up, the tribes of the LORD, to praise the name of the LORD according to the statute given to Israel.

Psalm 125:2 As the mountains surround Jerusalem, so the LORD surrounds his people both now and forevermore.

Psalm 126 When the LORD brought back the captives to Zion, we were like men who dreamed. Our mouths were filled with laughter, our tongues with songs of joy. Then it was said among the nations, "The LORD has done great things for them." The LORD has done great things for us, and we are filled with joy. Restore our fortunes, O LORD, like streams in the Negev. Those who sow in tears will reap with songs of joy. He who goes out weeping, carrying seed to sow, will return with songs of joy, carrying sheaves with him.

Psalm 127:1 Unless the LORD builds the house, its builders labor in vain. Unless the LORD watches over the city, the watchmen stand guard in vain.

Psalm 128:5-6 May the LORD bless you from Zion all the days of your life; may you see the prosperity of Jerusalem, and may you live to see your children's children. Peace be upon Israel.

Psalm 130:7-8 O Israel, put your hope in the LORD, for with the LORD is unfailing love and with him is full redemption. He himself will redeem Israel from all their sins.

Psalm 135:4 For the LORD has chosen Jacob to be his own, Israel to be his treasured possession.

Psalm 135:12 And he gave their land as an inheritance, an inheritance to his people Israel.

Psalm 136:21-22 And gave their land as an inheritance, His love endures forever, an inheritance to his servant Israel; His love endures forever.

Psalm 137:4-6 How can we sing the songs of the LORD while in a foreign land? If I forget you, O Jerusalem, may my right hand forget its skill. May my tongue cling to the roof of my mouth if I do not remember you, if I do not consider Jerusalem my highest joy.

Psalm 147:2-3 The LORD builds up Jerusalem; he gathers the exiles of Israel. He heals the brokenhearted and binds up their wounds.

Isaiah 10:21-22 A remnant will return, a remnant of Jacob will return to the Mighty G-d. Though your people, O Israel, be like the sand by the sea, only a remnant will return.

Isaiah 11:11-12 In that day the LORD will reach out his hand a second time to reclaim the remnant that is left of his people from Assyria, from Lower Egypt, from Upper Egypt, from Cush, from Elam, from Babylonia, from Hamath and from the islands of the sea. He will raise a banner for the nations and gather the exiles of Israel; He will assemble the scattered people of Judah from the four quarters of the earth.

Isaiah 14:1-2 The LORD will have compassion on Jacob [Israel]; once again he will choose Israel and will settle them in their own land. Aliens will join them and unite with the house of Jacob. Nations will take them and bring them to their own place. And the house of Israel will possess the nations as menservants and maidservants in the LORD'S land.

Isaiah 27:12-13 In that day the LORD will thresh from the flowing Euphrates to the Wadi of Egypt, and you, O Israelites, will be gathered up one by one. And in that day a great trumpet will sound. Those who were perishing in Assyria and those who were exiled in Egypt will come and worship the LORD on the holy mountain in Jerusalem.

Isaiah 35:10 And the ransomed of the LORD will return. They will enter Zion with singing; everlasting joy will crown their heads. Gladness and joy will overtake them, and sorrow and sighing will flee away.

Isaiah 41:8-10 But you, O Israel, my servant, Jacob, whom I have chosen, you descendants of Abraham my friend, I took you from the ends of the earth, from its farthest corners I called you. I said, "You are my servant"; I have chosen you and have not rejected you. So do not fear, for I am with you; do not be dismayed, for I am your G-d. I will strengthen you and help you; I will uphold you with my righteous right hand.

Isaiah 43:5-6 Do not be afraid, for I am with you; I will bring your children from the east and gather you from the west. I will say to the north, "Give them up!" and to the south, "Do not hold them back." Bring my sons from afar and my daughters from the ends of the earth.

Isaiah 44:21-22 Remember these things, O Jacob, for you are my servant, O Israel. I have made you, you are my servant; O Israel, I will not forget you. I have swept away your offenses like a cloud, your sins like the morning mist. Return to me, for I have redeemed you.

Isaiah 43:16-19 This is what the LORD says— he who made a way through the sea, a path through the mighty waters, who drew out the chariots and horses, the army and reinforcements together, and they lay there, never to rise again, extinguished, snuffed out like a wick: Forget the former things; do not dwell on the past. See, I am doing a new thing! Now it springs up; do you not perceive it?

Isaiah 44:26 Who carries out the words of his servants and fulfills the predictions of his messengers, who says of Jerusalem, "It shall be inhabited," of the towns of Judah, "They shall be built," and of their ruins, "I will restore them."

Isaiah 45:20 Gather together and come; assemble, you fugitives from the nations.

Isaiah 46:3-4 Listen to me, O house of Jacob, all you who remain of the house of Israel, you whom I have upheld since you were conceived, and have carried since your birth. Even to your old age and gray hairs I am he, I am he who will sustain you. I have made you and I will carry you; I will sustain you and I will rescue you.

Isaiah 48:20 Leave Babylon, flee from the Babylonians! Announce this with shouts of joy and proclaim it. Send it out to the ends of the earth; say, "The LORD has redeemed his servant Jacob."

Isaiah 49:5-6 And now the LORD says—he who formed me in the womb to be his servant to bring Jacob back to him and gather Israel to himself, for I am honored in the eyes of the LORD and my G-d has been my strength—he says: "It is too small a thing for you to be my servant to restore the tribes of Jacob and bring back those of Israel I have kept. I will also make you a light for the Gentiles, that you may bring my salvation to the ends of the earth."

Isaiah 49:11-12 I will turn all my mountains into roads, and my highways will be raised up. See, they will come from afar—some from the north, some from the west, some from the region of Sinim.

Isaiah 49:14-18 But Zion said, "The LORD has forsaken me, the LORD has forgotten me." Can a mother forget the baby at her breast and have no compassion on the child she has borne? Though she may forget, I will not forget you! See, I have engraved you on the palms of my hands; your walls are ever before me. Your sons hasten back, and those who laid you waste depart from you. Lift up your eyes and look around; all your sons gather and come to you. "As surely as I live," declares the LORD, "You will wear them all as ornaments; you will put them on, like a bride."

Isaiah 49:19-20 Though you were ruined and made desolate and your land laid waste, now you will be too small for your people, and those who devoured you will be far away. The children born during your bereavement will yet say in your hearing, "This place is too small for us; give us more space to live in."

Isaiah 49:22 This is what the Sovereign LORD says: "See, I will beckon to the Gentiles, I will lift up my banner to the peoples; they will bring your sons in their arms and carry your daughters on their shoulders."

Isaiah 51:3 The LORD will surely comfort Zion and will look with compassion on all her ruins; he will make her deserts like Eden, her wastelands like the garden of the LORD. Joy and gladness will be found in her, thanksgiving and the sound of singing.

Isaiah 51:11 The ransomed of the LORD will return. They will enter Zion with singing; everlasting joy will crown their heads. Gladness and joy will overtake them, and sorrow and sighing will flee away.

Isaiah 52:2-3 Shake off your dust; rise up, sit enthroned, O Jerusalem. Free yourself from the chains on your neck, O captive Daughter of Zion. For this is what the LORD says: "You were sold for nothing, and without money you will be redeemed."

Isaiah 52:11-12 Depart, depart, go out from there! Touch no unclean thing! Come out from it and be pure, you who carry the vessels of the LORD. But you will not leave in haste or go in flight; for the LORD will go before you, The G-d of Israel will be your rear guard.

Isaiah 54:3 For you will spread out to the right and to the left; your descendants will dispossess nations and settle in their desolate cities.

Isaiah 54:6-8 "The LORD will call you back as if you were a wife deserted and distressed in spirit—a wife who married young, only to be rejected," says your G-d. "For a brief moment I abandoned you, but with deep compassion I will bring you back. In a surge of anger I hid my face from you for a moment, but with everlasting kindness I will have compassion on you," says the LORD your Redeemer.

Isaiah 56:6-8 And foreigners who bind themselves to the LORD to serve him, to love the name of the LORD, and to worship him, all who keep the Sabbath without desecrating it and who hold fast to my covenant—these I will bring to my holy mountain and give them joy in my house of prayer. Their burnt offerings and sacrifices will be accepted on my altar; for my house will be called a house of prayer for all nations. The Sovereign LORD declares—he who gathers the exiles of Israel: "I will gather still others to them besides those already gathered."

Isaiah 57:13 When you cry out for help, let your collection of idols save you! The wind will carry all of them off, a mere breath will blow them away. But the man who makes me his refuge will inherit the land and possess my holy mountain.

Isaiah 58:12 Your people will rebuild the ancient ruins and will raise up the age- old foundations; you will be called Repairer of Broken Walls, Restorer of Streets with Dwellings.

Isaiah 58:14 "Then you will find your joy in the LORD, and I will cause you to ride on the heights of the land and to feast on the inheritance of your father Jacob." The mouth of the LORD has spoken.

Isaiah 60:4-5 Lift up your eyes and look about you: All assemble and come to you; your sons come from afar, and your daughters are carried on the arm. Then you will look and be radiant, your heart will throb and swell with joy; the wealth on the seas will be brought to you, to you the riches of the nations will come.

Isaiah 61:4-7 They will rebuild the ancient ruins and restore the places long devastated; they will renew the ruined cities that have been devastated for generations. Aliens will shepherd your flocks; foreigners will work your fields and vineyards. And you will be called priests of the LORD, you will be named ministers of our G-d. You will feed on the wealth of nations, and in their riches you will boast. Instead of their shame my people will receive a double portion, and instead of disgrace they will rejoice in their inheritance; and so they will inherit a double portion in their land, and everlasting joy will be theirs.

Isaiah 62 For Zion's sake I will not keep silent, for Jerusalem's sake I will not remain quiet, till her righteousness shines out like the dawn, her salvation like a blazing torch. The nations will see your righteousness, and all kings your glory; you will be called by a new name that the mouth of the LORD will bestow. You will be a crown of splendor in the LORD'S hand, a royal diadem in the hand of your G-d. No longer will they call you Deserted, or name your land Desolate. But you will be called Hephzibah, and your land Beulah; for the LORD will take delight in you, and your land will be married. As a young man marries a maiden, so will your sons marry you; as a bridegroom rejoices over his bride, so will your G-d rejoice over you. I have posted watchmen on your walls, O Jerusalem; they will never be silent day or night. You who call on the LORD, give yourselves no rest, and give him no rest till he establishes Jerusalem and makes her the praise of the earth. The LORD has sworn by his right hand and by his mighty arm: "Never again will I give your grain as food for your enemies, and never again will foreigners drink the new wine for which you have toiled; but those who harvest it will eat it and praise the LORD, and those who gather the grapes will drink it in the courts of my sanctuary." Pass through, pass through the gates! Prepare the way for the people. Build up, build up the highway! Remove the stones. Raise a banner for the nations. The LORD has made proclamation to the ends of the earth: "Say to the Daughter of Zion, 'See, your Savior comes! See, his reward is with him and his recompense accompanies him.'" They will be called The Holy People, The Redeemed of the LORD; and you will be called Sought After, The City No Longer Deserted.

Isaiah 63:17-18 Why, O LORD, do you make us wander from your ways and harden our hearts so we do not revere you? Return for the sake of your servants, the tribes that are your inheritance. For a little while your people possessed your holy place, but now our enemies have trampled down your sanctuary.

Isaiah 65:9 I will bring forth descendants from Jacob, and from Judah those who will possess my mountains, my chosen people will inherit them, and there will my servants live.

Isaiah 66:8-10 Who has ever heard of such a thing? Who has ever seen such things? Can a country be born in a day or a nation be brought forth in a moment? Yet no sooner is Zion in labor than she gives birth to her children. Do I bring to the moment of birth and not give delivery?" says the LORD. "Do I close up the womb when I bring to delivery?" says your G-d. Rejoice with Jerusalem and be glad for her, all you who love her; rejoice greatly with her, all you who mourn over her.

Isaiah 66:18 And I, because of their actions and their imaginations, am about to come and gather all nations and tongues, and they will come and see my glory.

Isaiah 66:20-22 "And they will bring all your brothers, from all the nations to my holy mountain in Jerusalem as an offering to the LORD— on horses, in chariots and wagons, and on mules and camels," says the LORD. "They will bring them, as the Israelites bring their grain offerings to the temple of the LORD in ceremonially clean vessels." And I will select some of them also to be priests and Levites," says the LORD. "As the new heavens and the new earth that I make will endure before me," declares the LORD, "so will your name and descendants endure."

Jeremiah 3:14-18 "Return, faithless people," declares the LORD, "for I am your husband. I will choose you--one from a town and two from a clan--and bring you to Zion. Then I will give you shepherds after my own heart, who will lead you with knowledge and understanding. In those days, when your numbers have increased greatly in the land," declares the LORD, "Men will no longer say, 'The ark of the covenant of the LORD.' It will never enter their minds or be remembered; it will not be missed, nor will another one be made. At that time they will call Jerusalem The Throne of the LORD, and all nations will gather in Jerusalem to honor the name of the LORD. No longer will they follow the stubbornness of their evil hearts. In those days the house of Judah will join the house of Israel, and together they will come from a northern land to the land I gave your forefathers as an inheritance."

Jeremiah 4:5-6 Announce in Judah and proclaim in Jerusalem and say: "Sound the trumpet throughout the land!" Cry aloud and say: "Gather together! Let us flee to the fortified cities!" Raise the signal to go to Zion! Flee for safety without delay! For I am bringing disaster from the north, even terrible destruction.

Jeremiah 12:14-15 This is what the LORD says: "As for all my wicked neighbors who seize the inheritance I gave my people Israel, I will uproot them from their lands and I will uproot the house of Judah from among them. But after I uproot them, I will again have compassion and will bring each of them back to his own inheritance and his own country."

Jeremiah 16:14-15 "However, the days are coming," declares the LORD, "when men will no longer say, 'As surely as the LORD lives, who brought the Israelites up out of Egypt,' but they will say, 'As surely as the LORD lives, who brought the Israelites up out of the land of the north and out of all the countries where he had banished them.' For I will restore them to the land I gave their forefathers."

Jeremiah 23:3-6 "I myself will gather the remnant of my flock out of all the countries where I have driven them and will bring them back to their pasture, where they will be fruitful and increase in number. I will place shepherds over them who will tend them, and they will no longer be afraid or terrified, nor will any be missing," declares the LORD. "The days are coming," declares the LORD, "when I will raise up to David a righteous Branch, a King who will reign wisely and do what is just and right in the land. In his days Judah will be saved and Israel will live in safety. This is the name by which he will be called: The LORD Our Righteousness."

Jeremiah 23:7-8 "So then, the days are coming," declares the LORD, "when people will no longer say, 'As surely as the LORD lives, who brought the Israelites up out of Egypt,' but they will say, 'As surely as the LORD lives, who brought the descendants of Israel up out of the land of the north and out of all the countries where he had banished them.' Then they will live in their own land."

Jeremiah 24:6-7 My eyes will watch over them for their good, and I will bring them back to this land. I will build them up and not tear them down; I will plant them and not uproot them. I will give them a heart to know me, that I am the LORD. They will be my people, and I will be their G-d, for they will return to me with all their heart.

Jeremiah 27:22 "They will be taken to Babylon and there they will remain until the day I come for them," declares the LORD. "Then I will bring them back and restore them to this place."

Jeremiah 29:11-14 "For I know the plans I have for you," declares the LORD, "plans to prosper you and not to harm you, plans to give you hope and a future. Then you will call upon me and come and pray to me, and I will listen to you. You will seek me and find me when you seek me with all your heart. I will be found by you," declares the LORD, "and will bring you back from captivity. I will gather you from all the nations and places where I have banished you," declares the LORD, "and will bring you back to the place from which I carried you into exile."

Jeremiah 30:3 "The days are coming," declares the LORD, "when I will bring my people Israel and Judah back from captivity and restore them to the land I gave their forefathers to possess," says the LORD.

Jeremiah 30:10 "So do not fear, O Jacob my servant; do not be dismayed, O Israel," declares the LORD, "I will surely save you out of a distant place, your descendants from the land of their exile. Jacob will again have peace and security, and no one will make him afraid."

Jeremiah 31:8-9 See, I will bring them from the land of the north and gather them from the ends of the earth. Among them will be the blind and the lame, expectant mothers and women in labor; a great throng will return. They will come with weeping; they will pray as I bring them back.

I will lead them beside streams of water on a level path where they will not stumble, because I am Israel's father, and Ephraim is my firstborn son.

Jeremiah 31:10-11 Hear the word of the LORD, O nations; proclaim it in distant coastlands; He who scattered Israel will gather them and will watch over his flock like a shepherd. For the LORD will ransom Jacob and redeem them from the hand of those stronger than they.

Jeremiah 31:12 They will come and shout for joy on the heights of Zion; They will rejoice in the bounty of the LORD—the grain, the new wine and the oil, the young of the flocks and herds. They will be like a well-watered garden, and they will sorrow no more.

Jeremiah 31:15-17 This is what the LORD says: "A voice is heard in Ramah mourning and great weeping, Rachel weeping for her children and refusing to be comforted because her children are no more." This is what the LORD says: "Restrain your voice from weeping and your eyes from tears, for your work will be rewarded," declares the LORD. "They will return from the land of the enemy. So there is hope for your future," declares the LORD. "Your children will return to their own land."

Jeremiah 31:21-22 Set up road signs; put up guideposts. Take note of the highway, the road that you take. Return, O Virgin Israel, return to your towns. How long will you wander, O unfaithful daughter?

Jeremiah 31:23-25 This is what the LORD Almighty, the G-d of Israel, says: "When I bring them back from captivity, the people in the land of Judah and in its towns will once again use these words: 'The LORD bless you, O righteous dwelling, O sacred mountain.' People will live together in Judah and all its towns—farmers and those who move about with their flocks. I will refresh the weary and satisfy the faint."

Jeremiah 31:27-28 "The days are coming," declares the LORD, "when I will plant the house of Israel and the house of Judah with the offspring of men and of animals. Just as I watched over them to uproot and tear down, and to overthrow, destroy and bring disaster, so I will watch over them to build and to plant," declares the LORD.

Jeremiah 32:37-41 I will surely gather them from all the lands where I banish them in my furious anger and great wrath; I will bring them back to this place and let them live in safety. They will be my people, and I will be their G-d. I will give them singleness of heart and action, so that they will always fear me for their own good and the good of their children after them. I will make an everlasting covenant with them: I will never stop doing good to them, and I will inspire them to fear me, so that they will never turn away from me. I will rejoice in doing them good and will assuredly plant them in this land with all my heart and soul.

Jeremiah 33:7 I will bring Judah and Israel back from captivity and will rebuild them as they were before.

Jeremiah 33:14 "The days are coming," declares the LORD, "when I will fulfill the gracious promise I made to the house of Israel and to the house of Judah."

Jeremiah 46:16 They will stumble repeatedly; they will fall over each other. They will say, "Get up, let us go back to our own people and our native lands, away from the sword of the oppressor."

Jeremiah 46:27 Do not fear, O Jacob my servant; do not be dismayed, O Israel. I will surely save you out of a distant place, your descendants from the land of their exile. Jacob will again have peace and security, and no one will make him afraid.

Jeremiah 50:3-5 A nation from the north will attack her and lay waste her land. No one will live in it; both men and animals will flee away. "In those days, at that time," declares the LORD, " the people of Israel and the people of Judah together will go in tears to seek the LORD their G-d. They will ask the way to Zion and turn their faces toward it. They will come and bind themselves to the LORD in an everlasting covenant that will not be forgotten."

Jeremiah 50:19 But I will bring Israel back to his own pasture and he will graze on Carmel and Bashan; his appetite will be satisfied on the hills of Ephraim and Gilead.

Jeremiah 50:33-34 This is what the LORD Almighty says: "The people of Israel are oppressed, and the people of Judah as well. All their captors hold them fast, refusing to let them go. Yet their redeemer is strong; the LORD Almighty is his name. He will vigorously defend their cause so that he may bring rest to their land, but unrest to those who live in Babylon.

Jeremiah 51:5-6 For Israel and Judah have not been forsaken by their G-d, the LORD Almighty, though their land is full of guilt before the Holy One of Israel. Flee from Babylon! Run for your lives! Do not be destroyed because of her sins. It is time for the LORD'S vengeance, he will pay her what she deserves.

Jeremiah 51:33 This is what the LORD Almighty, the G-d of Israel, says: "The Daughter of Babylon is like a threshing floor at the time it is trampled; the time to harvest her will soon come."

Jeremiah 51:45 Come out of her, my people! Run for your lives! Run from the fierce anger of the LORD.

Jeremiah 51:50 You who have escaped the sword, leave and do not linger! Remember the LORD in a distant land, and think on Jerusalem.

Lamentations 4:22 O daughter of Zion your punishment will end; he will not prolong your exile.

Ezekiel 11:16-17 Therefore say: "This is what the Sovereign LORD says: Although I sent them far away among the nations and scattered them among the countries, yet for a little while I have been a sanctuary for them in the countries where they have gone." Therefore say, "This is what the Sovereign LORD says: I will gather you from the nations and bring you back from the countries where you have been scattered, and I will give you back the land of Israel again.

Ezekiel 20:34-38 I will bring you from the nations and gather you from the countries where you have been scattered--with a mighty hand and an outstretched arm and with outpoured wrath. I will bring you into the desert of the nations and there, face to face, I will execute judgement upon you. As I judged your fathers in the desert of the land of Egypt, so I will judge you, declares the Sovereign LORD. I will take note of you as you pass under my rod, and I will bring you into the bond of the covenant. I will purge you of those who revolt and rebel against me. Although I will bring them out of the land where they are living, yet they will not enter the land of Israel. Then you will know that I am the LORD.

Ezekiel 20:41-42 I will accept you as fragrant incense when I bring you out from the nations and gather you from the countries where you have been scattered, and I will show myself holy among you in the sight of the nations. Then you will know that I am the LORD, when I bring you into the land of Israel, the land I had sworn with uplifted hand to give to your fathers.

Ezekiel 28:25 This is what the Sovereign LORD says: When I gather the people of Israel from the nations where they have been scattered, I will show myself holy among them in the sight of the nations. Then they will live in their own land, which I gave to my servant Jacob.

Ezekiel 34:13 I will bring them out from the nations and gather them from the countries, and I will bring them into their own land.

Ezekiel 36 "Son of man, prophesy to the mountains of Israel and say, 'O mountains of Israel, hear the word of the LORD. This is what the Sovereign LORD says: The enemy said of you "Aha! The ancient heights have become our possession."' Therefore prophesy and say, 'This is what the Sovereign LORD says: Because they ravaged and hounded you from every side so that you became the possession of the rest of the nations and the object of people's malicious talk and slander, therefore, O mountains of Israel, hear the word of the Sovereign LORD: This is what the Sovereign LORD says to the mountains and hills, to the ravines and valleys, to the desolate ruins and the deserted towns that have been plundered and ridiculed by the rest of the nations around you--this is what the Sovereign LORD says: In my burning zeal I have spoken against the rest of the nations, and against all Edom, for with glee and with malice in their hearts they made my land their own possession so that they might plunder its pastureland.' Therefore prophesy concerning the land of Israel and say to the mountains and hills, to the ravines and valleys: 'This is what the Sovereign LORD says: I speak in my jealous wrath because you have suffered the scorn of the nations. Therefore this is what the Sovereign LORD says: I swear with uplifted hand that the nations around you will also suffer scorn.

"'But you, O mountains of Israel, will produce branches and fruit for my people Israel, for they will soon come home. I am concerned for you and will look on you with favor; you will be plowed and sown, and I will multiply the number of people upon you, even the whole house of

Israel. The towns will be inhabited and the ruins rebuilt. I will increase the number of men and animals upon you, and they will be fruitful and become numerous. I will settle people on you as in the past and will make you prosper more than before. Then you will know that I am the LORD. I will cause people, my people Israel, to walk upon you. They will possess you, and you will be their inheritance; you will never again deprive them of their children.

"'This is what the Sovereign LORD says: Because people say to you, "You devour men and deprive your nation of its children," therefore you will no longer devour men or make your nation childless, declares the Sovereign LORD. No longer will I make you hear the taunts of the nations, and no longer will you suffer the scorn of the peoples or cause your nation to fall, declares the Sovereign LORD.'"

Again the word of the LORD came to me: "Son of man, when the people of Israel were living in their own land, they defiled it by their conduct and their actions. Their conduct was like a woman's monthly uncleanness in my sight. So I poured out my wrath on them because they had shed blood in the land and because they had defiled it with their idols. I dispersed them among the nations and they were scattered through the countries; I judged them according to their conduct and their actions. And wherever they went among the nations they profaned my holy name, for it was said of them, 'These are the LORD'S people, and yet they had to leave his land.' I had concern for my holy name, which the house of Israel profaned among the nations where they had gone.

"Therefore say to the house of Israel, 'This is what the Sovereign LORD says: It is not for your sake, O house of Israel, that I am going to do these things, but for the sake of my holy name, which you have profaned among the nations where you have gone. I will show the holiness of my great name, which has been profaned among the nations, the name you have profaned among them. Then the nations will know that I am the LORD, declares the Sovereign LORD, when I show myself holy through you before their eyes.

"'For I will take you out of the nations; I will gather you from all the countries and bring you back into your own land. I will sprinkle clean water on you, and you will be clean; I will cleanse you from all your impurities and from all your idols. I will give you a new heart and put a new spirit in you; I will remove from you your heart of stone and give you a heart of flesh. And I will put my Spirit in you and move you to follow my decrees and be careful to keep my laws. You will live in the land I gave your forefathers; you will be my people, and I will be your G-d. I will save you from all your uncleanness. I will call for the grain and make it plentiful and will not bring famine upon you. I will increase the fruit of the trees and the crops of the field, so that you will no longer suffer disgrace among the nations because of famine. Then you will remember your evil ways and wicked deeds, and you will loathe yourselves for your sins and detestable practices. I want you to know that I am not doing this for your sake, declares the Sovereign LORD. Be ashamed and disgraced for your conduct, O house of Israel!

"'This is what the Sovereign LORD says: On the day I cleanse you from all your sins, I will resettle your towns, and the ruins will be rebuilt. The desolate land will be cultivated instead of lying desolate in the sight of all who pass through it. They will say, "This land that was laid waste has become like the garden of Eden; the cities that were lying in ruins, desolate and destroyed, are now fortified and inhabited." Then the nations around you that remain will know that I the LORD have rebuilt what was destroyed and have replanted what was desolate. I the LORD have spoken and I will do it.'

"This is what the Sovereign LORD says: Once again I will yield to the plea of the house of Israel and do this for them: I will make their people as numerous as sheep, as numerous as the flocks for offerings at Jerusalem during her appointed feasts. So will the ruined cities be filled with flocks of people. Then they will know that I am the LORD."

Ezekiel 37 The hand of the LORD was upon me, and he brought me out by the Spirit of the LORD and set me in the middle of a valley; it was full of bones. He led me back and forth among them, and I saw a great many bones on the floor of the valley, bones that were very dry. He asked me, "Son of man, can these bones live?"

I said, "O Sovereign LORD, you alone know."

Then he said to me, "Prophesy to these bones and say to them, 'Dry bones, hear the word of the LORD! This is what the Sovereign LORD says to these bones: I will make breath enter you, and you will come to life. I will attach tendons to you and make flesh come upon you and cover you with skin; I will put breath in you, and you will come to life. Then you will know that I am the LORD.'"

So I prophesied as I was commanded. And as I was prophesying, there was a noise, a rattling sound, and the bones came together, bone to bone. I looked, and tendons and flesh appeared on them and skin covered them, but there was no breath in them.

Then he said to me, "Prophesy to the breath; prophesy, son of man, and say to it, 'This is what the Sovereign LORD says: Come from the four winds, O breath, and breathe into these slain, that they may live.'" So I prophesied as he commanded me, and breath entered them; they came to life and stood up on their feet--a vast army.

Then he said to me: "Son of man, these bones are the whole house of Israel. They say, 'Our bones are dried up and our hope is gone; we are cut off.' Therefore prophesy and say to them: 'This is what the Sovereign LORD says: O my people, I am going to open your graves and bring you up from them; I will bring you back to the land of Israel. Then you, my people, will know that I am the LORD, when I open your graves and bring you up from them. I will put my Spirit in you and you will live, and I will settle you in your own land. Then you will know that I the LORD have spoken, and I have done it, declares the LORD.'"

The word of the LORD came to me: "Son of man, take a stick of wood and write on it, 'Belonging to Judah and the Israelites associated with him.' Then take another stick of wood, and write on it, 'Ephraim's stick, belonging to Joseph and all the house of Israel associated with him.' Join them together into one stick so that they will become one in your hand.

"When your countrymen ask you, 'Won't you tell us what you mean by this?' say to them, 'This is what the Sovereign LORD says: I am going to take the stick of Joseph--which is in Ephraim's hand--and of the Israelite tribes associated with him, and join it to Judah's stick, making them a single stick of wood, and they will become one in my hand.' Hold before their eyes the sticks you have written on and say to them, 'This is what the Sovereign LORD says: I will take the Israelites out of the nations where they have gone. I will gather them from all around and bring them back into their own land. I will make them one nation in the land, on the mountains of Israel. There will be one king over all of them and they will never again be two nations or be divided into two kingdoms. They will no longer defile themselves with their idols and vile images or with any of their offenses, for I will save them from all their sinful backsliding, and I will cleanse them. They will be my people, and I will be their G-d.

"'My servant David will be king over them, and they will all have one shepherd. They will follow my laws and be careful to keep my decrees. They will live in the land I gave to my servant Jacob, the land where your fathers lived. They and their children and their children's children will live there forever, and David my servant will be their prince forever. I will make a covenant of peace with them; it will be an everlasting covenant. I will establish them and increase their numbers, and I will put my sanctuary among them forever. My dwelling place will be with them; I will be their G-d, and they will be my people. Then the nations will know that I the LORD make Israel holy, when my sanctuary is among them forever.'"

Ezekiel 37:21-22 This is what the Sovereign LORD says: "I will take the Israelites out of the nations where they have gone. I will gather them from all around and bring them back into their own land. I will make them one nation in the land, on the mountains of Israel. There will be one king over all of them and they will never again be two nations or be divided into two kingdoms.

Ezekiel 38:8 (Regarding Gog) After many days you will be called to arms. In future years you will invade a land that has recovered from war, whose people were gathered from many nations to the mountains of Israel, which had long been desolate. They had been brought out from the nations, and now all of them live in safety.

Ezekiel 39:25-29 Therefore this is what the Sovereign LORD says: "I will now bring Jacob back from captivity; and will have compassion on all the people of Israel, and I will be zealous for my holy name. They will forget their shame and all the unfaithfulness they showed toward me when they lived in safety in their land with no one to make them afraid. When I have brought them back from the nations and have gathered them from the countries of their enemies, I will show myself holy through them in the sight of many nations. Then they will know that I am the LORD their G-d, for though I sent them into exile among the nations, I will gather them to their own land, not leaving any behind. I will no longer hide my face from them, for I will pour out my Spirit on the house of Israel, declares the Sovereign LORD.

Ezekiel 45-48 Division of the Land, Offerings and Holy Days, Boundaries, gates of the city.

Ezekiel 47:13-14 This is what the Sovereign LORD says: "These are the boundaries by which you are to divide the land for an inheritance among the twelve tribes of Israel, with two portions for Joseph. You are to divide it equally among them. Because I swore with uplifted hand to give it to your forefathers, this land will become your inheritance.

Daniel 12 (Deliverance of the Jewish people in the last days) At that time Michael [the Archangel], the great prince who protects your people will arise.

Hosea 1:10-11 Yet the Israelites will be like the sand on the seashore, which cannot be measured or counted. In the place where it was said to them, "You are not my people," they will be called "sons of the living G-d." The people of Judah and the people of Israel will be reunited, and they will appoint one leader and will come up out of the land, for great will be the day of Jezreel.

Hosea 3:4-5 For the Israelites will live many days without king or prince, without sacrifice or sacred stones, without ephod or idol. Afterward the Israelites will return and seek the LORD their G-d and David their king. They will come trembling to the LORD and to his blessings in the last days.

Hosea 6:11 Also for you, Judah, a harvest is appointed. Whenever I would restore the fortunes of my people.

Hosea 8:10 Although they have sold themselves among the nations, I will now gather them together.

Hosea 11:1 When Israel was a child, I loved him, and out of Egypt I called my son.

Hosea 14:1 Return, O Israel, to the LORD your G-d.

Hosea 14:7 Men will dwell again in his shade. He will flourish like the grain. He will blossom like a vine, and his fame will be like the wine from Lebanon.

Joel 2:18-19 Then the LORD will be jealous for his land and take pity on his people. The LORD will reply to them: "I am sending you grain, new wine and oil, enough to satisfy you fully; never again will I make you an object of scorn to the nations."

Joel 2:32 And everyone who calls on the name of the LORD will be saved; for on Mount Zion and in Jerusalem there will be deliverance, as the LORD has said, among the survivors whom the LORD calls.

Joel 3:1-2 In those days and at that time, when I restore the fortunes of Judah and Jerusalem I will gather all nations and bring them down to the Valley of Jehoshaphat. There I will enter into judgement against them concerning my inheritance, my people Israel, for they scattered my people among the nations and divided up my land.

Joel 3:14-16 Multitudes, multitudes in the valley of decision! For the day of the LORD is near in the valley of decision. The sun and moon will be darkened, and the stars no longer shine. The LORD will roar from Zion and thunder from Jerusalem; the earth and the sky will tremble, but the LORD will be a refuge for his people, a stronghold for the people of Israel.

Joel 3:20 Judah will be inhabited forever and Jerusalem through all generations.

Amos 2:10 I brought you up out of Egypt, and I led you forty years in the desert to give you the land of the Amorites.

Amos 5:4 This is what the LORD says to the house of Israel: "Seek me and live."

Amos 9:14-15 "I will bring back my exiled people Israel; they will rebuild the ruined cities and live in them. They will plant vineyards and drink their wine; they will make gardens and eat their fruit. I will plant Israel in their own land never again to be uprooted from the land I have given them," says the LORD your G-d.

Obadiah 1:17,19 But on Mount Zion will be deliverance; it will be holy, and the house of Jacob will possess its inheritance. People from the Negev will occupy the mountains of Esau, and people from the foothills will possess the land of the Philistines. They will occupy the fields of Ephraim and Samaria, and Benjamin will possess Gilead.

Obadiah 1:20-21 This company of Israelite exiles who are in Canaan will possess the land as far as Zarephath; the exiles from Jerusalem who are in Sepharad will possess the towns of the Negev. Deliverers will go up on Mount Zion to govern the mountains of Esau. And the kingdom will be the LORD'S.

Jonah 2:8 Those who cling to worthless idols forfeit the grace that could be theirs.

Micah 2:12-13 I will surely gather all of you, O Jacob; I will surely bring together the remnant of Israel. I will bring them together like sheep in a pen, like a flock in its pasture; the place will throng with people. One who *breaks open the way* will go up before them; they will break through the gate and go out. Their king will pass through before them, the LORD at their head.

Micah 4:1-2 In the last days the mountain of the LORD'S temple will be established as chief among the mountains; it will be raised above the hills, and peoples will stream to it. Many nations will come and say, "Come, let us go up to the mountain of the LORD, to the house of the G-d of Jacob. He will teach us his ways, so that we may walk in his paths." The law will go out from Zion, the word of the LORD from Jerusalem.

Micah 4:6-7 "In that day," declares the LORD, "I will gather the lame; I will assemble the exiles and those driven away a strong nation. The lord will rule over them in Mount Zion from that day and forever."

Micah 4:10-13 Writhe in agony, O Daughter of Zion, like a woman in labor, for now you must leave the city to camp in the open field. You will go to Babylon; there you will be rescued. There the LORD will redeem you out of the hand of your enemies. But now many nations are gathered against you. They say, "Let her be defiled, let our eyes gloat over Zion!" But they do not know the thoughts of the LORD; they do not understand his plan, he who gathers them like sheaves to the threshing floor. "Rise and thresh, O Daughter of Zion, for I will give you horns of iron; I will give you hoofs of bronze and you will break to pieces many nations." You will devote their ill-gotten gains to the LORD, their wealth to the LORD of all the earth.

Micah 5:2-4 But you, Bethlehem Ephratha, though you are small among the clans of Judah, out of you will come for me one who will be ruler over Israel, whose origins are from of old, from ancient times. Therefore Israel will be abandoned until the time when she who is in labor gives birth and the rest of his brothers return to join the Israelites.

Micah 7:14-15 Shepherd your people with your staff, the flock of your inheritance, which lives by itself in a forest, in fertile pasturelands. Let them feed in Bashan and Gilead as in days long ago. "As in the days when you came out of Egypt, I will show them my wonders."

Micah 7:18-20 Who is a G-d like you, who pardons sin and forgives the transgression of the remnant of his inheritance? You do not stay angry forever but delight to show mercy. You will again have compassion on us; you will tread our sins underfoot and hurl all our iniquities into the depths of the sea. You will be true to Jacob, and show mercy to Abraham, as you pledged on oath to our fathers in days long ago.

Nahum 1:15 Look, there on the mountains, the feet of one who brings good news, who proclaims peace. Celebrate your festivals, O Judah, and fulfill your vows. No more will the wicked invade you; they will be completely destroyed.

Zephaniah 2:1-2 Gather together, gather together, O shameful nation, before the appointed time arrives and that day sweeps on like chaff, before the fierce anger of the LORD comes upon you, before the day of the LORD'S wrath comes upon you.

Zephaniah 2:9 "Therefore, as surely as I live," declares the LORD Almighty, the G-d of Israel, "surely Moab will become like Sodom, the Ammonites like Gomorrah--a place of weeds and salt pits, a wasteland forever. The remnant of my people will plunder them; the survivors of my nation will inherit their land."

Zephaniah 3:8 "Therefore wait for me," declares the LORD, "for the day I will stand up to testify. I have decided to assemble the nations, to gather the kingdoms and to pour out my wrath on them--all my fierce anger. The whole world will be consumed by the fire of my jealous anger."

Zephaniah 3:19-20 At that time I will deal with all who opposed you; I will rescue the lame and gather those who have been scattered. I will give them praise and honor in every land where they were put to shame. "At that time I will gather you: at that time I will bring you home. I will give you honor and praise among all the peoples of the earth when I restore your fortunes before your very eyes" says the LORD.

Haggai 2:6-9 This is what the LORD Almighty says: "In a little while I will once more shake the heavens and the earth, the sea and the dry land. I will shake all nations, and the desired of all nations will come, and I will fill this house with glory," says the LORD Almighty. "The silver is mine and the gold is mine," declares the LORD Almighty. "The glory of this present house will be greater than the glory of the former house," says the LORD Almighty. "And in this place I will grant peace," declares the LORD Almighty.

Zechariah 2:6-7 "Come! Come! Flee from the land of the north," declares the LORD, "for I have scattered you to the four winds of heaven" declares the LORD. "Come, O Zion! Escape, you who live in the Daughter of Babylon!"

Zechariah 2:10-13 "Shout and be glad, O Daughter of Zion. For I am coming, and I will live among you," declares the LORD. "Many nations will be joined with the LORD in that day and will become my people. I will live among you and you will know that the LORD Almighty has sent me to you. The LORD will inherit Judah as his portion in the holy land and will again choose Jerusalem. Be still before the LORD, all mankind, because he has roused himself from his holy dwelling."

Zechariah 8:7-8 This is what the LORD Almighty says: "I will save my people from the countries of the east and the west. I will bring them back to live in Jerusalem; they will be my people, and I will be faithful and righteous to them as their G-d."

Zechariah 8:13 As you have been an object of cursing among the nations, O Judah and Israel, so will I save you, and you will be a blessing. Do not be afraid, but let your hands be strong.

Zechariah 8:20-23 This is what the LORD Almighty says: "Many peoples and the inhabitants of many cities will yet come, and the inhabitants of one city will go to another and say, 'Let us go at once to entreat the LORD and seek the LORD Almighty. I myself am going.' And many peoples and powerful nations will come to Jerusalem to seek the LORD Almighty and to entreat him." This is what the LORD Almighty says: "In those days ten men from all languages and nations will take firm hold of one Jew by the edge of his robe and say, 'Let us go with you, because we have heard that G-d is with you.'"

Zechariah 9:16 The LORD their G-d will save them on that day as the flock of his people. They will sparkle in his land like jewels in a crown.

Zechariah 10:6 I will strengthen the house of Judah and save the house of Joseph. I will restore them because I have compassion on them. They will be as though I had not rejected them, for I am the LORD their G-d and I will answer them.

Zechariah 10:8-10 I will signal for them and gather them in. Surely I will redeem them; they will be as numerous as before. Though I scatter them among the peoples, yet in distant lands they will remember me. They and their children will survive, and they will return. I will bring them back from Egypt and gather them from Assyria. I will bring them to Gilead and Lebanon, and there will not be room enough for them.

Zechariah 13:8-9 "In the whole land," declares the LORD, "two-thirds will be struck down and perish; yet one-third will be left in it. This third I will bring into the fire; I will refine them like silver and test them like gold. They will call on my name and I will answer them; I will say, 'They are my people,' and they will say, 'The LORD is our G-d.'"

Zechariah 14:14 Judah too will fight at Jerusalem. The wealth of all the surrounding nations will be collected--great quantities of gold and silver and clothing.

Zechariah 14:16 Then the survivors from all the nations that have attacked Jerusalem will go up year after year to worship the King, the LORD Almighty, and to celebrate the Feast of Tabernacles.

Appendix B
Zionist Documents

The Basel Program

This was the basic document of the Jewish national revival. It was formulated at the First Zionist Congress, which took place in Basel, Switzerland in August 1897, and was accepted as the policy of the movement until the establishment of an independent State of Israel in 1948.

Zionism strives to create for the Jewish people a home in Palestine secured by public law.

The Congress contemplates the following means to the attainment of this end:

1. The promotion, on suitable lines, of the colonization of Palestine by Jewish agricultural and industrial workers.

2. The organization and binding together of the whole of Jewry by means of appropriate institutions, local and international, in accordance with the laws of each country.

3. The strengthening and fostering of Jewish national sentiment and consciousness.

4. Preparatory steps towards obtaining Government consent, where necessary, to the attainment of the aim of Zionism.

"In Basel I Founded the Jewish State"

This is an excerpt from Theodore Herzl's diary for September 3, 1897. He had just returned to Vienna after the Congress, and this is how he assessed its achievements.

Were I to sum up the Basel Congress in a word—which I shall guard against pronouncing publicly—it would be this: At Basel I founded the Jewish State.

If I said this out loud today, I would be answered by universal laughter. Perhaps in five years, and certainly fifty, everyone will know it. The foundation of a State lies in the will of the people for a State, yes, even in the will of one sufficiently powerful individual (l'Etat c'est moi--Louis XIV). Territory is only the material basis; the State, even when it possesses territory, is always something abstract. The Church State exists even without it; otherwise the Pope would not be sovereign.

At Basel, then, I created this abstraction which, as such, is invisible to the vast majority of people. And with infinitesimal means, I gradually worked the people into the mood for a State and made them feel that they were its National Assembly.

The Balfour Declaration

This was Britain's statement of sympathy with Zionism during World War I. There were many drafts, and the final version is a careful compromise that eschewed an exact definition of what was intended by the term "National Home," and it was at the root of much subsequent controversy.

Foreign Office,

November 2nd, 1917

Dear Lord Rothschild,

I have much pleasure in conveying to you, on behalf of His Majesty's Government, the following declaration of sympathy with Jewish Zionist aspirations which has been submitted to, and approved by, the Cabinet.

> His Majesty's Government views with favour the establishment in Palestine of a national home for the Jewish people, and will use their best endeavours to facilitate the achievement of this object, it being clearly understood that nothing shall be done which may prejudice the civil and religious rights of existing non-Jewish communities in Palestine, or the rights and political status enjoyed by Jews in any other country.

I should be grateful if you would bring this declaration to the knowledge of the Zionist Federation.

Yours sincerely,
Arthur James Balfour

The Proclamation of Independence

This was read by David Ben-Gurion on May 14, 1948, in a small building then being used as the town museum in Tel Aviv. Signatories to the Declaration were the thirty-seven members of the Provisional State Council.

The Land of Israel was the birthplace of the Jewish people. Here their spiritual, religious and national identity was formed. Here they achieved independence and created a culture of national and universal significance. Here they wrote and gave the Bible to the world.

Exiled from the Land of Israel, the Jewish people remained faithful to it in all the countries of their dispersion, never ceasing to pray and hope for their return and the restoration of their national freedom.

Impelled by this historic association Jews strove throughout the centuries to go back to the land of their fathers and regain their statchood. In recent decades they returned in their masses. They reclaimed the wilderness, revived their language, built cities and villages and established a vigorous and ever-growing community, with its own economic and cultural life. They sought peace yet were prepared to defend themselves. They brought the blessings of progress to all inhabitants of the country and looked forward to sovereign independence.

In the year 1897 the First Zionist Congress, inspired by Theodore Herzl's vision of the Jewish State, proclaimed the right of the Jewish people to national revival in their own country.

This right was acknowledged by the Balfour Declaration of November 2, 1917, and re-affirmed by the Mandate of the League of Nations, which gave explicit international recognition to the historic connection of the Jewish people with Palestine and their right to reconstitute their National Home.

The recent Holocaust, which engulfed millions of Jews in Europe, proved anew the need to solve the problem of the homelessness and lack of independence of the Jewish people by means of the re-establishment of the Jewish State, which would open the gates to all Jews and endow the Jewish people with equality of status among the family of nations.

The survivors of the disastrous slaughter in Europe, and also Jews from other lands, have not desisted from their efforts to reach *Eretz*-Israel, in face of difficulties, obstacles and perils; and have not ceased to urge their right to a life of dignity, freedom and honest toil in their ancestral land.

In the Second World War the Jewish people in Palestine made their full contribution to the struggle of the freedom-loving nations against the Nazi evil. The sacrifices of their soldiers and their war effort gained them the right to rank with the nations which founded the United Nations.

On November 29, 1947, the General Assembly of the United Nations adopted a Resolution requiring the establishment of a Jewish State in Palestine. The General Assembly called upon the inhabitants of the country to take all the necessary steps on their part to put the plan into effect. This recognition by the United Nations of the right of the Jewish people to establish their independent State is unassailable.

It is the natural right of the Jewish people to lead, as do all other nations, an independent existence in its sovereign State.

ACCORDINGLY WE, the members of the National Council, representing the Jewish people in Palestine, and the World Zionist Movement, are met together in solemn assembly today, the day of termination of the British Mandate for Palestine; and by virtue of the natural and historic right of the Jewish people and of the Resolution of the General Assembly of the United Nations.

WE HEREBY PROCLAIM the establishment of the Jewish State in Palestine, to be called "Medinat Israel" (The State of Israel).

WE HEREBY DECLARE that, as from the termination of the Mandate at midnight, the 14th-15th May, 1948, and pending the setting up of the duly elected bodies of the state in accordance with a Constitution, to be drawn up by the Constituent Assembly not later than the 1st October, 1948, the National Council shall act as the Provisional State Council, and that the National Administration shall constitute the Provisional Government of the Jewish State, which shall be known as Israel.

THE STATE OF ISRAEL will be open to the immigration of Jews from all countries of their dispersion; will promote the development of the country for the benefit of all its inhabitants; will be based on the principles of liberty, justice and peace as conceived by the prophets of Israel, will uphold the full social and political equality of all its citizens, without distinction of religion, race or sex; will guarantee freedom of religion, conscience, education and culture; will safeguard the Holy Places of all religions; and will loyally uphold the principles of the United Nations Charter.

THE STATE OF ISRAEL will be ready to cooperate with the organs and representatives of the Untied Nations in the implementation of the Resolution of the Assembly of November 29, 1947, and will take steps to bring about the Economic Union over the whole of Palestine.

We appeal to the United Nations to assist the Jewish people in the building of its State and to admit Israel into the family of nations.

In the midst of wanton aggression, we yet call upon the Arab inhabitants of the State of Israel to preserve the ways of peace and play their part in the development of the State, on the basis of full and equal citizenship and due representation in all its bodies and institutions--provisional and permanent.

We extend our hand in peace and neighborliness to all the neighboring states and their peoples, and invite them to cooperate with the independent Jewish nation for the common good of all. The State of Israel is prepared to make its contribution to the progress of the Middle East as a whole.

Our call goes out to the Jewish people all over the world to rally to our side in the task of immigration and development and to stand by us in the great struggle for the fulfillment of the dream of generations of the redemption of Israel.

With trust in Almighty G-d, we set our hand to this Declaration, at this Session of the Provisional State Council, on the soil of the Homeland, in the city of Tel Aviv, on this Sabbath eve, the fifty of Iyar, 5708, the fourteenth day of May, 1948.

(The signatories) David Ben-Gurion, Daniel Auster, Mordechai Bentov, Isaac Ben-Zvi, Eliyahu Berligne, Fritz (Peretz) Bernstein, Rabbi Wolf Gold, Meir Grabovsky, Isaac Gruenbaum, Dr. Abraham Granovsky (Granott), Eliyahu Dobkin, Meir Wilner-Kovner, Zerach Wahrhaftig, Herzl Vardi, Rachel Cohen,

Rabbi Kalman Kahana, Saadia Kobashi, Rabbi Isaac Meir Levin, Meir David Loewenstein, Zvi Luria, Golda Myerson (Meir), Nachum Nir, Zvi Segal, Rabbi Yehuda Leib Fishman (Maimon), David Zvi Pinkas, Aharon Zisling, Moshe Kolodny (Kol), Eliezer Kaplan, Abraham Katznelson, Felix Rosenblueth (Rosen), David Remez, Berl Repetur, Mordechai Schattner, Ben Zion Sternberg, Bechor Shitreet, Moshe Shapira, Moshe Shertok (Sharett).

Appendix C

Jewish Population Statistics in the USA

To help you pray for, warn and otherwise assist the Jewish people return to Israel.

Jewish Population of the United States by State

	Estimated Jewish Population**	Total Population*	Jewish Percent of Total
Alabama	9,000	4,662,000	0.2
Alaska	3,000	686,000	0.5
Arizona	106,000	6,500,000	1.7
Arkansas	2,000	2,855,000	0.1
California	1,194,000	36,757,000	3.3
Colorado	88,000	4,939,000	1.8
Connecticut	113,000	3,501,000	3.2
Delaware	15,000	873,000	1.8
District of Columbia	28,000	592,000	4.8
Florida	655,000	18,328,000	3.6
Georgia	127,000	9,686,000	1.4
Hawaii	7,000	1,288,000	0.5
Idaho	1,000	1,524,000	0.1
Illinois	279,000	12,902,000	2.2
Indiana	17,000	6,377,000	0.3
Iowa	6,000	3,003,000	0.2
Kansas	18,000	2,802,000	0.7
Kentucky	11,000	4,269,000	0.3
Louisiana	10,000	4,411,000	0.2
Maine	14,000	1,316,000	1.1
Maryland	235,000	5,311,000	4.2
Massachusetts	258,000	6,498,000	4.0
Michigan	87,000	10,003,000	0.9
Minnesota	47,000	5,220,000	0.9
Mississippi	2,000	2,939,000	0.1
Missouri	59,000	5,912,000	1.0

Montana	1,000	967,000	0.1
Nebraska	7,000	1,783,000	0.4
Nevada	70,000	2,600,000	2.8
New Hampshire	10,000	1,316,000	0.8
New Jersey	479,000	8,683,000	5.5
New Mexico	11,000	1,984,000	0.6
New York	1,618,000	19,490,000	8.4
North Carolina	28,000	9,222,000	0.3
North Dakota	450	641,000	0.1
Ohio	145,000	11,486,000	1.3
Oklahoma	5,000	3,642,000	0.1
Oregon	32,000	3,790,000	0.9
Pennsylvania	285,000	12,448,000	2.3
Rhode Island	19,000	1,051,000	1.8
South Carolina	11,000	4,480,000	0.3
South Dakota	300	804,000	(z)
Tennessee	19,000	6,215,000	0.3
Texas	130,000	24,327,000	0.6
Utah	4,000	2,736,000	0.2
Vermont	6,000	621,000	0.9
Virginia	98,000	7,769,000	1.3
Washington	43,000	6,549,000	0.7
West Virginia	2,000	1,814,000	0.1
Wisconsin	28,000	5,628,000	0.5
Wyoming	400	533,000	0.1
Total	6,444,000	307,233,000	2.2

Totals may not be exact due to rounding.

*Resident population, July 1, 2008 (Source: US Bureau of the Census).

**Resident population, 2007 (Source: American Jewish Committee, New York, NY, American Jewish Year Book)

(z) Figure is less than 0.1 and rounds to 0.

Appendix D

Investing in Israel

—Real Estate

Buy a house or apartment in Israel for investment and fire insurance for when things get worse in the USA to be prepared in Israel your homeland.

Some generally reliable Real Estate Agents:

Anglo Saxon Real Estate

15 Brazil St.
Tel-Aviv, 61392
Israel
Phone +972 (3) 642-8772
Fax +972 (3) 642-8323
Email: headofce@anglo_saxon.co.il
www.israel-real-estate.co.il/NewHome_E.asp

ReMax

Impact Properties
Bareket Building
Airport City P.O.B. 126
Ben Gurion 70100
Phone +972 (3) 972-0660
Fax +972 (3) 972-0661
Contact: Bernard Riskin, Regional Director
Email: reisrael@netvision.net.il
www.remax-israel.com

—Israeli Bonds

Invest in Israeli Bonds to Support Jewish Immigration and The State of Israel in Other Ways. Returns up to 5.9% (Dec. 2003).

General Info:

Israel bonds are securities issued by the State of Israel to help ongoing absorption of new immigrants, and build and strengthen the nation's economy and infrastructure. Projects include aiding the construction of the Trans-Israel Highway, the building of desalinization plants, expansion of transportation links, Jerusalem's light rail system, and a Tel Aviv subway system. In the USA, Israel Bonds are available through the Development Corporation for Israel (est. 1951), a New York corporation and a NASD-registered broker-dealer. Offices of the Development Corporation for Israel are located throughout the USA.

How to Invest:

Contact the local Israel Bonds office in your area. To find the local office in your area either contact the National Headquarters listed below or check the web-site www.israelbonds.com. A registered representative in your area will provide you with a prospectus and assist you through the investment process.

Rates of most of the securities are adjusted on the first of each month. Check the Israel Bonds web-site or contact your local Israel Bonds office to get the current rates.

In USA Contact:

Development Corporation for Israel / State of Israel Bonds

National Headquarters
575 Lexington Ave. Suite 600
New York, New York 10022
Phone (212) 644-BOND
Contact: Any Account Representative
webmaster@israelbonds.com

In Canada Contact:

Development Corporation for Israel / State of Israel Bonds

970 Lawrence Avenue West, Suite 502
Toronto, Ontario, M6A 3B6
Phone (416) 789-3351
Fax (416) 789-9436
Contact: Any Account Representative
Email: toronto@israelbonds.ca
www.israelbonds.ca

—Make *Aliyah*
Who to Apply to for *Aliyah* and Where.

Jewish Agency
http://www.jaif.org.il,   Email: elibir@jazo.org
Helping establish a modern state of Israel by providing services for new immigrants to Israel.

Nefesh B'nefesh
7200 West Camino Real, Suite 101
Boca Raton, FL 33433
Phone (561) 955-1908
Fax (561) 955-9850
Email: info@nefeshbnefesh.org
Assisting Jews immigrate to Israel through services, grants, and loans.

Tehilla
New York, USA
633 Third Ave, 21st Floor
New York, New York 10017-6706
Phone (212) 339-6055
Fax (212) 318-6145
Email: ny@tehilla.com

Israel Aliyah Center

633 Third Avenue, 21ˢᵗ Floor
New York, New York 10017-6706
Phone (212) 339-6063
Fax (212) 318-6145
Email: *aliyah*@jazo.org.il
http:// www.*aliyah*.org
Professional Schlichim assist in the step-by-step *Aliyah* process.

Kumah

http:// www.kumah.org
Encouraging and facilitating mass *Aliyah* to Israel.

The author is not available to do press-conferences or interviews about this book, but remains praying for the Jewish people to follow the seven hundred scriptures in this book and to contact Jewish agencies, like the ones mentioned in this book, to help them invest in and come home to Israel.